Social
Science

DATE DUE

THE FIRST 100 DAYS OF THE KENNEDY ADMINISTRATION

LET US BEGIN

Commentary by

MARTIN AGRONSKY

ERIC F. GOLDMAN

SIDNEY HYMAN

BARBARA WARD

WALLACE WESTFELDT, JR.

IRA WOLFERT

Photographs by Magnum

CORNELL CAPA

HENRI CARTIER-BRESSON

ELLIOTT ERWITT

BURT GLINN

CONSTANTINE MANOS

INGE MORATH

MARC RIBOUD

DENNIS STOCK

NICOLAS TIKHOMIROFF

SIMON AND SCHUSTER / NEW YORK / 1961

PHOTOGRAPHIC EDITOR: CORNELL CAPA

COMPOSITION BY THE COMPOSING ROOM, INC., NEW YORK
TEXT PRINTED BY ART COLOR PRINTING, DUNELLEN, N.J.
COVER PRINTED BY KIPE OFFSET PROCESS, NEW YORK

A Note for the Reader

THIS IS *a new kind of book.*

It began in a spirit of excitement only ten days after President Kennedy took office. Within a week, writers were in Washington talking to key Administration officials; photographers were working in the Congo, in South America, in Laos and all over the United States. All of them had a single purpose: to report, analyze and interpret the essential meaning of the events happening in the first days of the new Administration. Their words and pictures are focused on history while that history is being made; they are not concerned with "spot" news, nor can they assume the perspective of the classical historian's insight. Theirs is the story of the United States and the world as faced by the Kennedy Administration in its first 100 days.

No one connected with the book has any illusions about the finality of these "100 days." The year 1961 is not 1933, or 1861, or 1781—and the President himself was the first to point out the futility of looking for miraculous instant answers to America's problems or the world's uneasiness.

But with a view to the ultimate possibility of answers, and with a classic Inaugural Address still echoing, the Kennedy Administration has moved off to a fast and fascinating start. The "new generation" of men in Washington (and the men and women sent by them around the world) have plunged into their jobs with a verve and dedication that have made them the most talked-about and most closely observed officials who have ever taken national office.

While it would be unfair to measure the Kennedy Administration's first weeks against promises of immediate and total accomplishment, it nevertheless seems appropriate to document the circumstances, good and bad, in which it is making its earnest beginnings.

To this end, two groups of uniquely qualified men and women have brought this book into being. The photographers, who can often work where writers are barred admission, have captured the vital moments and what they stand for: a Government food package being passed into the hands of an unemployed miner, an Ecuadorian mother drinking the water out of a new pump from the United States, a Presidential assistant on Capitol Hill urging a Congressman to support a Kennedy proposal. For their part, the writers have gone beyond the moment, searching the past and the future for the central purpose behind each idea, each Executive move, each announced program, in an effort to illumine the way the Administration is defining its goals and moving toward them.

The result is an appraisal of the men who are now governing the United States, those who are governed by them, and the peoples of the rest of the world who look to them with new hope. As such, it is dedicated to the same principle established by President Kennedy when he promised:

"For my part, I shall withhold from neither the Congress nor the people any fact or report past, present or future which is necessary for an informed judgment of our conduct and hazards..."

M. LINCOLN SCHUSTER
Publisher

RICHARD L. GROSSMAN
Editor

Contents

Jacket photograph by Cornell Capa

"... *the torch has been passed to a new generation of Americans* ..."

NEW GENERATION

by ERIC F. GOLDMAN / Photographed by CORNELL CAPA

AFTER THE Inaugural Address, Dwight Eisenhower got rid of his tall silk topper, changed to his favorite homburg, drifted off with some friends to a luncheon at the 1925 F Street Club. How did it feel to be an ex-President? people kept asking him. "Great, fine," Eisenhower would reply, but beyond that he had little to say. It was not his day. It was not, emphatically, to be his kind of Administration.

The outgoing President believed that the Chief Executive should not attempt to run things too much and especially should not try to whiplash Congress and the nation into line. John Kennedy took office with whip brandished high. His models were the rambunctious Republican Theodore Roosevelt and the herd-riding Democrats Woodrow Wilson and Franklin Roosevelt. Shortly before Inauguration Day, he was reading with enthusiasm the book of a Columbia professor, Richard E. Neustadt, entitled *Presidential Power*, the theme of which was bluntly announced as "personal power and its politics: what it is, how to get it, how to keep it, how to use it." For a President to rule, action was necessary, and a swirl of action came from Kennedy's first hours in the White House. He hurried out into the January chill, hatless and coatless, to greet his first caller, Harry Truman, witnessed the collective swearing in of the Cabinet, fired off more nominations to the Senate, made his presence felt at a Democratic National Committee meeting, issued Executive Order No. I ordering Secretary of Agriculture Orville Freeman to double the rations of surplus foods provided to some 4,000,000 needy Americans. Incessantly Kennedy phoned, took calls, popped in and out of his office. That night the lights burned late all across the Executive buildings of Washington. In the Kennedy Administration, said Secretary of Labor Arthur J. Goldberg, "the deadline for everything is day before yesterday."

Amid the whirligig, the President took specific institutional steps to see to it that he ruled. Promptly he abolished the office that Sherman Adams had held; nobody was going to stand between him and his aides and the public. Almost as quickly he abolished the top-level Operations Coordinating Board set up by Eisenhower to bring together activities dealing with foreign policy. The President, said the Executive Order, intended to maintain "direct communications with the responsible agency so that everyone will know what I have decided." He further ordered the discontinuance of seventeen interdepartmental agencies, sixteen of them set up under Eisenhower. The directive saved more than $300,000 a year, but, as Presidential Press Secretary Pierre Salinger pointed out, economy was not the primary motive. The agencies were eliminated to "clarify and pinpoint executive responsibility."

Before long it was clear that Kennedy was using Cabinet meetings primarily as a symbolic institution. The Cabinet was meeting far less than under Eisenhower and making fewer collective decisions. The decisions were being made by John Kennedy alone, after consultation with individual departmental heads and other aides and after a relentless gathering of facts. Each Department was instructed to send detailed reports to the White House twice a week. In addition, a liaison man was established in every Department, and, depending on what kind of issue was urgent, one of these men might be contacted by the White House two or three times a day. "I never heard of a President who wanted to know so much," the State Department adviser Charles Bohlen remarked, and the whole capital soon agreed. At an early press conference, Kennedy answered in a detailed way a question that involved a proposed shipment to the United States of $12,000,000 worth of Cuban molasses. The reporters gasped. The information had appeared four days earlier, down near the bottom of one of the Departmental reports.

Kennedy was so determined to keep control of things that more than one observer guessed he was resorting to the practice President Franklin Roosevelt had perfected—setting up conflicting and competing centers of power within his Administration to keep everybody on his toes and to see to it that no one became too entrenched. The most suggestive situation was in the most critical area—foreign policy. Across town from the White House, in an awesome office in the new State Department building, Secretary of State Dean Rusk was duly installed, but just a tunnel's walk from the White House, in the old State Department building, was the brilliant McGeorge Bundy with the highly flexible instruction to concern himself with "national security matters" and the decided practice of popping in and out of the President's office. Some commentators wondered whether Dean Rusk was not in danger of becoming the Cordell Hull of the Kennedy Administration, and McGeorge Bundy was not in a position where he could be the Harry Hopkins.

A good deal of the activity of the Kennedy Administration was politics—plain old-fashioned politics. Early in Eisenhower's first term a questioner had asked him how he liked politics and the President frowned. "Being President," he said, "is a very fascinating experience, but the word 'politics'—I have no great liking for that." Asked to comment on this quote, Kennedy snapped, "I do have a great liking for the word 'politics.' It's the

Moments after the President's
State of the Union Message:
politics as usual.

way a President gets things done." The new President himself was endlessly receiving politicians. He or his aides were endlessly telephoning politicians, and the calls were not offhand. In the second-floor White House office of Lawrence F. O'Brien, special assistant to the President for "personnel and Congressional liaison," was a card file containing the background of every Senator and Representative. Among the details were the Congressman's close friends, his college fraternity, his wife's maiden name, his economic and educational milieu—information that has its uses. A tough, candid operator, O'Brien made it a point to talk over the President's program in detail with Congressional delegations, adding that the White House would call Congressmen with good news for constituents and the offices of Cabinet members would report unpleasant news. Congressmen quickly learned that when a man voted against the President, more and more of the news came from the Cabinet.

Amid all the glittering appointments Kennedy was making, there were also the careful political pay-offs—most blatantly, the handout to Governor John M. Patter-

son of Alabama, who had declared for Kennedy when the South was still showing a notable resistance to his nomination. Patterson wanted a high-ranking job for his close political associate, Charles M. Meriwether, and the President named Meriwether a director of the Export-Import Bank. Republicans and some newspapers cried shame. The Export-Import Bank is an important agency that often deals with Asiatic and African nations. Meriwether was an acknowledged segregationist and onetime campaign manager for John Crommelin in a campaign marked by racist and anti-Semitic doctrines. Kennedy stuck by the appointment and the heavy Democratic majority in the Senate dutifully confirmed it.

At a press conference, a reporter brought up the Meriwether case.

He was confident, the President said, that Meriwether would do a "good job." And with that politico Kennedy pointed to the next questioner.

In the political maneuverings, in the policy making, in many of the day-by-day workings of the Administration, always and everywhere there was John Kennedy. "Under our system of government," he had once remarked, "the President is everything or he is nothing." This President, quite clearly, did not intend to be nothing. To increase the impact of his press conferences, he permitted live telecasts—the first in American history—and let it be known that he also intended to go on TV on a number of other occasions as soon as he had worked out the most effective format. In his first sixty days in office, Kennedy sent to Congress twenty-nine messages and more than a score of draft bills; addressed twenty-eight communications to foreign leaders; made twelve public speeches; took a hand in answering an amazingly large number of the 30,000 letters that were flooding the White House every week. Now and again he even dropped in on Departmental meetings—sitting, chin in hand, listening closely and occasionally joining in the discussion.

Nothing was overlooked, including the attractiveness and bounce of the Kennedy family, to increase the President's hold on Washington and on general public opinion. Three-year-old Caroline Kennedy was beguiling as only a three-year-old can be, and newsmen were given full access to her activities. Everybody knew that when Truman came visiting the second time, Caroline stood grinning in her royal blue overalls and white sweater and her father had to nudge her. "What did I tell you to tell him?" "Oh, yes, you used to live in our house." And everybody knew how Caroline had gone wandering into the White House communications room one Sunday and, when a reporter asked, "What is your Daddy doing?" she said, "Oh, he's upstairs, with his shoes and socks off, doing nothing."

When the Caroline news ran thin, there were always the endless other Kennedys doing things. Soon the newspapers were carrying the story about Robert F. Kennedy, Jr., the seven-year-old son of the President's brother, the Attorney General. Bobby, it seems, had sent the President a note: "Dear Jack, I WOuld like To see

YOU Soon by Jack." Bobby showed up at the White House every inch a news item, gray flannel suit neatly pressed, hair tousled, and carrying a seven-inch salamander, with black and yellow spots, in a glass vase.

"What is it?" asked the President as the flash bulbs went off.

"I don't know what it is. I caught it in the pool. They bite."

The President stirred the vase with a stick and the salamander turned over. "God, he's turned over," the President said. "What do you call him?"

"Shadrach," said Bobby, to the delight of millions of readers.

THE TRADE PAPERS of the fashion industry were featuring a different story. Women's shops across the country reported that customers were coming in by the thousands and asking for the "Kennedy suit," the "Kennedy coat," or especially the "Kennedy hat." But in areas like Fairfield County, Connecticut, specialty shops wanted no part of wholesalers who pushed "the Jackie Kennedy look." She wouldn't dare try to sell the clothes, one owner explained. "I'd lose the sale and probably the customer too."

The waspishness of the wives of the brokers and advertising men was only partly a result of partisan Republicanism. Jacqueline Bouvier Kennedy, she of the Dresden exquisiteness, so chic, so obviously the cosmopolitan socialite, was rapidly becoming a symbol, second in importance only to the President himself, not only of a way of dressing but also of a way of life.

Dwight Eisenhower's Washington had been the middle-class dream. The President headed a party which has spoken for decades with the accent of the business deal, the church supper, the golf course. Eisenhower liked the middle-class values, the middle-class manner, the middle-class joke. As he used to say, he enjoyed having those middle-class heroes, the successful businessmen, around him; their very success showed their high quality. They were around him in droves—as advisers and friends—and their attitudes seeped through the whole of Washington.

The opposition Democratic Party has been a peculiar institution in modern America. It has been, *par excellence*, the party of the poor or at least of the disadvantaged. But sometimes on the local level and much more on the national level, it has been led by people of the topmost social group. Eisenhower's first Secretary of the Treasury, George Humphrey, once remarked with almost as much accuracy as irritation, "The Democratic Party is led by men who inherited their money; the Republican Party, by men who made it themselves." Franklin Roosevelt, Adlai Stevenson, John Kennedy— all have been aristocrats (or, in the case of Kennedy, so close to it that the difference is unimportant) and all have had the patrician view of the world.

The American aristocracy is hardly easy to generalize about, but the members of the group who go into public life on the Democratic side do usually show certain characteristics. They have a certain patrician sniffishness toward mere successful businessmen (as the aristocrat Teddy Roosevelt said, such people need "education and sound chastisement"), a sense of *noblesse oblige* toward the less fortunate, a strong bent toward learning and the arts, and an enormous sense of personal security which makes them quite ready to be part of the informal, the new, the spectacular.

The Kennedys were soon giving Washington the authentic patrician air. Jackie Kennedy had under way a redecoration of the White House with the aid of Mrs. Henry Parrish, 2d, of New York, and what was happening looked like a redecoration by Mrs. Henry Parrish, 2d, of New York. Out from the White House, in French, went a phone call to Bui Van Han, the Vietnamese chef of the French Ambassador to England, who has the reputation of making the most delectable sauces in Western civilization. M. Van Han cabled, "Sorry cannot make the trip to become your chef," but it was clear that the White House was to be no steak-and-potatoes establishment.

The next week Mrs. Kennedy began making good her promise to turn the White House into "a showcase of American art and history," starting by throwing open

to the public the beautiful Vermeil Collection of gold-finished chinaware. Gaily she talked of the parties she was going to have for artists and writers and of her plan to establish White House-sponsored prizes for literature and the arts. The President did not lag behind. His voracious reading was becoming a staple comment in magazine articles about him. He went on television to pay a tribute to his favorite poet, Robert Frost, and said: "There is a story that some years ago an interested mother wrote to a principal of a school, 'Don't teach my boy poetry, he's going to run for Congress.' I've never taken the view that the world of politics and the world of poetry are so far apart."

If the worlds of poetry and of politics remained a bit apart, the worlds of politics and of ideas did not. The Harvard professors came flooding into Washington until everybody was repeating James Reston's crack that "Harvard will have nothing left but Radcliffe when Kennedy gets through raiding his alma mater." (Others savored the definition of a "failure" in the new Washington: "A Yale man driving an Edsel with a Nixon sticker on it.") But the members of the new Administration also came from throughout the American world of ideas—Walter W. Heller, from the University of Minnesota, to serve as Chairman of the Council of Economic Advisers; University of Virginia Law School Professor Mortimer M. Caplin, to be Commissioner of Internal Revenue; Edward R. Murrow, one of the country's most respected TV commentators, to direct the United States Information Agency; and George F. Kennan, leader in intellectual circles on both sides of the Atlantic, to represent the United States as Ambassador to pivotal Yugoslavia. As long as anyone could remember, the post of Postmaster General in the Cabinet had been the special preserve of the old-school politician, undefiled by books, ideas or anybody's new frontier. In the Kennedy era, few were surprised when the Postmaster General turned out to be J. Edward Day, University of Chicago Phi Bete, Harvard Law School honor graduate, author of two books—one of them a novel, *Barthalf Street*, which had Republicans sniffing whether it wasn't a bit raffish to be sent through the United States mails.

And through it all ran an informality such as Washington had never known. This was an Administration touched from top to bottom by the youthfulness, the self-confidence, the zest-in-everything of the patrician White House. For decades protocol had held that, as Herbert Hoover put it, "the President of the United States never calls on anyone." President and Mrs. John Kennedy went visiting friends like any other young couple—one of the first times, to the home of a newspaper reporter, Rowland Evans, Jr., of the New York *Herald Tribune*. At the President's gay, bantering luncheon for Congressional leaders, Republican Senate Leader Everett Dirksen was observed showing to Kennedy a twenty-five-cent key marked "The White House —Back Door," which he had bought in a drugstore. He wouldn't have shown it to any other President, said Dirksen, but he had no hesitation in showing it to Kennedy. Reporters going to the White House to talk to an aide were likely to run into the President walking restlessly about the halls and, if the aide was busy, to be asked, "Why don't you come in the office for a while?"

One fine Saturday John Kennedy just upped and disappeared for three hours. Wouldn't Press Secretary Salinger try to find out where he was? the newsmen asked.

"I did make an attempt," said Salinger, "and nobody seems to know."

At the press conferences, in his talks with visitors, at dinner parties, the President was spraying everything with his quick, tart quips. Were all the newspapers talking about the rising influence of McGeorge Bundy? "I think I'll continue to have residual functions," said John Kennedy. He opened his first speech to a businessman's organization: "It would be premature to ask your support in the next election and it would be inaccurate to thank you for it in the past." After the appointment as Attorney General of his thirty-five-year-old brother,

who had never tried a case in court, the President observed: "I can't see that it's wrong to give him a little legal experience before he goes out to practice law." As for the old pro politician Clark Clifford, a top Truman aide and the man who took charge of the transition from Eisenhower to Kennedy, the President told a dinner party: "Clark is a wonderful fellow. In a day when so many are seeking a reward for what they contributed to the return of the Democrats to the White House, you don't hear Clark clamoring. He was invaluable to us, and all he asked in return was that we advertise his law firm on the backs of the one-dollar bills."

Soon the informality of the whole top Administration had Washington old-timers rubbing their eyes. McGeorge Bundy, forty-one, went hustling through the tunnel connecting his office and the White House looking like a cocky young Ivy League instructor. Secretary of Labor Goldberg, the second oldest man in the Cabinet at fifty-two, whirled around five states on an inspection of recession spots, startling unemployment offices by his sudden appearances and observing, "This is the way we'll be doing things." Ex-Governor of Michigan G. Mennen (Soapy) Williams, forty-nine, Assistant Secretary of State for African Affairs, took off for Africa, promptly had Western European chancelleries in an uproar by declaring that he believed in "Africa for the Africans." Unperturbed, his green polka-dot bow tie chipper as ever, Williams hurried on, joining with a group of Congolese schoolboys in rendering "Nobody Knows the Trouble I've Seen," dipping his finger into an African chicken dish with gooey sauce called "moambe," licking the finger, and pronouncing moambe "good stuff," stripping down and wading into the mud to help tribesmen build a dike.

Meanwhile visitors were noticing a football sitting on the fireplace mantle in the office of Attorney General Robert F. Kennedy. Their curiosity was promptly satisfied. Attorney General Kennedy, varsity end at Harvard, and Deputy Attorney General Byron R. White, Phi Bete, Rhodes Scholar, Yale Law honor graduate, and the "Whizzer" White who was everybody's All-American in 1937, liked to toss the football around while deliberating matters of jurisprudence.

LONG BEFORE the Kennedy Administration was a reality, far back in the strange West Virginia primary campaign, a special note had been sounded. The miners and the hill folk would gather, heirs to generations of bitter anti-Catholic feeling, and they would look at the Catholic Kennedy and mutter, "I don't know about voting against that young man. He reminds me of F.D.R." The campaigning for Kennedy by Franklin Roosevelt, Jr., was a smash success. To many a West Virginian the two men seemed natural together, and both recalled the leader of the 1930s who, as a miner in Boone County put it, "really cared about us nobodies."

Throughout the 1960 campaign and the early period of the Kennedy Presidency there was plenty to keep fresh the comparison with the days of F.D.R. Kennedy's choice of Lyndon Johnson as his Vice Presidential running mate was a repeat of the 1932 Roosevelt–Garner ticket—the more liberal, Northeastern No. 1 candidate and the more conservative, Southern No. 2 candidate. Midway in the campaign of 1960, in a speech to which the Democratic camp gave special emphasis, Kennedy heightened the comparison by pointing to the so-called "Hundred Days" which opened the New Deal. The way the Roosevelt Administration began, Kennedy declared, showed that "the first ninety days of the next President's Administration will be the crucial days," and that he, as President, proposed to act accordingly. Kennedy's victory pattern repeated the old F.D.R. coalition —the South plus the big cities of the North, with a special boost from the minorities of the big cities. And a thousand things, little and big, about the new Administration called up memories of the Roosevelt era—whether the general air of innovation or the President's zest in politicking, the onrush of intellectuals or the lights burning late all over Washington.

Yet 1961 was hardly 1933. John Kennedy had no landslide mandate from the American people. As a matter of fact, there were still plenty of Republicans growling that the handful of votes which separated Kennedy and Nixon had been stolen in the wards of Chicago. The United States, although worried by recession, was not in the fourth year of a depression which had put it in a mood where Will Rogers could say, "The whole country is with him [Roosevelt]. Even if what he does is wrong, they are with him. Just so he does something. If he burned down the Capitol, we would cheer and say, 'Well, we at least got a fire started anyhow.' " Instead the United States was, as Kennedy's intellectual friends had been emphasizing for a long time, in a mood of deep complacency. The Congress that came in with F.D.R. was so bewildered and frightened that Administration bills could be jammed down its throat with scarcely a whimper from them. (Not untypically, Roosevelt's banking legislation was debated by the House of Representatives for thirty-eight minutes and by the Senate for three hours.) The Congress that faced Kennedy was even more Republican than it had been under Eisenhower and just as influenced by a conservative Republican–Southern Democrat alliance. If Kennedy burned down the Capitol there would be millions—led by their Congressmen—to shriek, "I told you so."

Apart from any differences in specific practicalities, the oncoming era bore its own special mark. A Washington veteran caught the heart of the matter when he remarked, "No one could possibly say that this Kennedy Administration has much resemblance to the Eisenhower days. But whenever I hear it compared to the Roosevelt period, I'm uncomfortable. It's not that it's different in particular important ways—that isn't the real point. There's a much deeper, more subtle difference, something you have to call style or tone, or, as the sociologists like to say, a difference in its image of itself."

The subtle difference had been a long time in the making. Somewhere at the beginning of the twentieth century a strangely assorted group of Americans began to influence the national destiny. They were shaggy agrarians storming against the plutocracy of the East, Eastern aristocrats irritated at what the parvenu industrialists were doing to the country, little old ladies skittish at the thought of men working seventy hours a week, socialists with angry Utopias in their pockets, Single Taxers, labor unionists, progressives, syndicalists, not to speak of the rampant Theodore Roosevelt. They really had little in common—little except one potent idea. America was a very special place, something unique in all the history of man's aspirations. The uniqueness was not that the United States was a political democracy, where men could duly vote and even hod carriers could become Senators. The uniqueness was that America was the land of economic and social opportunity. And, the reformers went on, an alliance between the new industrialism and corrupt politics was seriously, outrageously, cutting down this opportunity for the ordinary man.

The reformers of the early twentieth century talked little about the rest of the world. Like most of the population of the United States, they assumed that the business of America was America. It was to get on with this business without dependence on other nations and without interference from them. At times, of course, there would be an interruption when some foreign nation, acting in a way that foreigners persist in acting, went berserk. Then the matter was to be settled by diplomacy or war but, whatever the technique, quickly and finally.

The reformers were the more inclined to believe in the quick, total solution of any world problem because they were so sure that the world was no great problem anyhow. They tended to assume a general international trend, a trend so certain that it took on the cast of a law of history. Human beings everywhere and at all times, the law ran, seek peace and democracy, want to get ahead to a farm of their own or a house on the right side of the tracks, prefer to do it gradually and with a decent regard for the amenities. The history of man is consequently a long, slow swing toward a world consisting entirely of middle-class democracies. Once in a while the trouble comes when some country falls under an evil leader who forces it along a road forbidden by the law of history. Then it is only necessary to remove the leader and let things flow back along their proper path. If such was the law of history itself, how could foreign policy be a problem requiring anything except the occasional surgical removal of an unnatural growth?

Behind all the attitudes of the reformers, in foreign or domestic affairs, was a faith, a credo so assumed that it rarely had to be spoken. Human beings are inherently good. Give the ordinary fellow a reasonable amount of opportunity, a sound house over his head, decent clothing, enough food so that tomorrow's dinner is not a constantly nagging problem, and he would emerge a balanced, kindly human being, quite interested in the general welfare.

Over the decades these American reformers continued to urge a vast variety of techniques to protect and broaden opportunity in the United States, but more and more they agreed on the use of governmental powers—particularly the powers of the Federal Government —as the most effective means. They continued to call themselves by a grab bag of names, but increasingly they were known as "liberals." The liberals scored continuing successes in the early twentieth century, were thrown back, broke into their heyday under the redoubtable Franklin Roosevelt. By the mid-1930s they were as cocky as F.D.R.'s uptilted cigarette about themselves and their doctrine—and they seemed to have every reason to be. When World War II came, most liberals broke with their old homeward-lookingness and took up some degree of internationalism in their thinking. But for only a few did this mean any basic reassessment of their ideas or of their faith, about America or about the world.

Then, suddenly, it happened. Liberals had hardly brushed the V-J confetti out of their hair when they were jolted by a hard fact. Something was decidedly wrong with their law of history. Around the world millions of men and women, far from moving gradually toward middle-class democracy, were hurtling off in an entirely different direction. Worse still, they were hurtling off in a way that threatened to bring into action the shockingly new fact of life—annihilation bombs.

Meanwhile, more gradually, the consummation of liberal dreams was bringing liberal nightmares. In post-World War II America, the great waves of prosperity kept rolling across the nation. Opportunity was everywhere. Jackie Robinson, dazzling the stands in his Dodgers uniform, was a flashing symbol of an era when for all poor men and for all minority groups the economic and social walls were coming tumbling down. And there he was now, the liberal's dream, the ordinary American, well housed, well fed, well clothed, freer from discriminations than all his ancestors—there he was, the liberal's dream and the center of a mass culture which could appall and frighten. The years of savage McCarthyism especially troubled liberals. For the bellowing Senator, a menace to everything reformers stood for, roused his most fervid support precisely in the part of the population which the liberals had labored so hard and so hopefully to uplift—the new middle classes.

Other liberal successes created still more liberal worries. The liberal now had his big government, big beyond the fondest wishes of the early 1900s, and it could haunt him. Even the Federal administrative commissions, through which big government was to do so much of its good work, recalled the words of the astute railroad attorney Richard Olney, commenting on the Interstate Commerce Commission when it was created far back in 1887. Olney told a railroad baron to cheer up, for the Commission "is, or can be made, of great use to the railroads.... [It can be employed as] a sort of

barrier between the railroad corporations and the people and a sort of protection against hasty and crude legislation hostile to railroad interests.... The part of wisdom is not to destroy the Commission, but to utilize it."

Since the turn of the century, the liberals, in the name of the general welfare, had been especially favorable toward the oppressed farmers and the downtrodden workingmen. Now the biggest American labor union was led by none other than Jimmy Hoffa. The farmer, more than likely, was making $10,000 a year and was ready with a pitchfork for anybody who talked about cutting his Federal subsidies in the name of the general welfare. Above all, the liberal had staked his hopes on the democratic process—"The cure for any ill of democracy," as generations of reformers said, "is more democracy." But in an era of highly organized political parties using intricate organization, huge sums of money, and public-relations techniques little different from the ways of selling soap, the faith in the sheer democratic process had become quaint, to be remembered, as one remembered Teddy Roosevelt's teeth, only in a haze of mezzotint sentimentality.

All during the post-World War II period of liberal disillusionment and rethinking, a new group was beginning to filter into positions of leadership in politics, the universities, business and the world of letters. Chronologically, as President Kennedy said in his Inaugural Address, they were men born in the twentieth century. But in a more important sense they were the sons of the New Deal, men who were just coming to maturity as the domestic New Deal slid into history. Their first real experiences were fighting World War II and living and thinking during the development of the East-West clash, Korea, McCarthyism, and the emergence of an affluent, intensely group-centered, banal America.

Very few of these new leaders were conservatives. Very few were liberals in any traditional sense of the word. (Most of them, if they did not blanch at being called liberals, also did not delight in the description.) The 1930s were the years of ebullient, confident, uncomplicated liberalism. Now a Post-Liberal Generation was coming into its own under Post-Liberal John Kennedy and giving to Washington a tone that was neither Dwight Eisenhower nor Franklin Roosevelt.

IN PART, the Post-Liberals are quite ready to follow the long-running liberal emphases. They seek to go on protecting and broadening opportunity in America and they depend heavily on government as their means. They keep a good deal of the ultimate liberal faith that human beings can be excellent, or at least better. In part—but beyond these fundamentals almost everything is different, especially in the nuances that mean so much.

In one important respect, the Post-Liberal Generation has stood traditional liberalism on its head. The center of concern is no longer America; the focus is on the world and America's relations to it. It is no accident that Roosevelt's first Inaugural was almost exclusively concerned with domestic affairs and that Kennedy's opening address largely discussed world relations. It is no accident that in the Washington of the 1930s the most cherished posts were in departments like Labor and Agriculture; in the 1960s, in the State Department and other foreign-policy divisions.

The foreign policy that the Post-Liberal Generation emphasizes so much breaks not only with the older liberal isolationism but also with the One Worldism of the World War II period. That, too, depended on the law of history and expected easy, total answers. The Post-Liberals rely on no law of history unless it is the law that life is tough, for nations as well as men. Their internationalism is unenchanted, pragmatic, touched with a melancholy sense of the infinite complexity of things, tremendously leery of making a wrong move. If at times they show a One Worldish enthusiasm, that is largely

because they literally believe there will be one world or none. They are eager to act less because they are sure what the next step should be than because they are certain that inaction is still more dangerous.

The emphasis in domestic affairs shows an equally important shift. Of course, the Kennedy Administration promptly made bread-and-butter moves, particularly by pushing legislation to combat the recession and by issuing Executive Orders to increase job opportunities for Negroes, but it did these things in a way which left the impression that it did not consider economics the nub of the national need. Well before the election of 1960, Arthur Schlesinger, Jr., found a phrasing for the changed concern. American liberalism, he wrote, had been "quantitative." But now, with quantitative success largely achieved in the affluent society, it should turn to the "qualitative" development of the individual. The whole Kennedyite emphasis on the intellectual is not simply a return to F.D.R.'s love of jousting with the expert and his respect for the cultivated. It also represents, quite plainly, a conviction that the man in Levittown should not live by bread alone, no matter how attractively packaged or how tasty the slices—and that if he does, the United States will pay for it by purblind foreign policy and domestic stagnation.

Closely connected with this swing to the qualitative is an attitude that might almost be called the moralistic. The F.D.R. era had been notably lacking in pulpit talk. It had a cocked-eye manner that permitted its devotees, like the writer Edgar Kemler, to exult: "With the repeal of prohibition [at the beginning of the New Deal], sin was returned to the jurisdiction of the churches where it belongs, and the present administration has shown little inclination to reclaim it." But the Post-Liberal Generation had lived through the challenge of Communism to American values and the sickening feeling that Americans may have few values left except the pursuit of money and status or, if they do, they are not quite sure what the values are. Its leaders are the men who had kept appealing for a sense of "national purpose" and they now proposed to try to find and assert it.

The most conspicuous idea in President Kennedy's Inaugural Address was the summons to Americans to break away from the gimme attitude and ask instead, What can I do for my country? The most original and, many thought, the most characteristic move of the early Kennedy days was the establishment of the Peace Corps, with its direct call for selflessness. There was nothing to get out of it, the President emphasized in his announcement. Over and over again, the Peace Corps' Director, R. Sargent Shriver, Kennedy's brother-in-law, hammered on the same point. The Corps would not make you draft-exempt; it offered no real pay. It offered only "difficult" and "dangerous" living and the opportunity for "service."

The new moralism is the more striking because it is accompanied by the most unabashed power-consciousness that the Capitol has ever known. Early in the Administration Robert Frost advised the President: "Poetry and power is the formula for an Augustan Age. But be more Irish than Harvard. Don't be afraid of power." The remark was directed to a thoroughly receptive audience. (As a matter of fact, Frost was soon saying that he had received a letter from Kennedy across which was scrawled "Power all the way.") If the Post-Liberal Generation has any one central preoccupation, it is power—"how to get it, how to keep it, how to use it," as Post-Liberal Richard Neustadt wrote. They are done with the sunny dreamings of early-1900s progressivism, done with the confidence of the New Dealers that the masses would carry things forward. They have seen power, skillfully organized in the Russian society, become a direct threat to the national security of the United States. They have watched power shifts, inadequately sensed by the liberals, turn America over to McCarthyism and to what they considered eight years of dangerous Eisenhowerism. They are students—and products—of the new managerial America, a managerial world that includes political campaigns and universities as well as business corporations, and they are acutely aware that a managerial world is one in which men and ideas are made or broken by subtle configurations of power. They are part of the swing of educated Americans to psychological and sociological ways of thinking

—with the implicit warning of this kind of thinking that all human beings are manipulated by a tangled variety of circumstances. They have their own ideas of good—and they intend, by a sharp sensitivity to power considerations, to manipulate men and things toward those ideas.

"Poetry and power," ideals, intellectualism, and a realism bordering on cynicism—the Post-Liberal Generation was bringing to Washington a mixed tone, one so mixed that it was akin to ambivalence. People noticed it especially as President Kennedy announced the Peace Corps. He was putting before the United States a program that in its way was just about as radically idealistic a proposal as has ever been presented to Americans —and he did it in an unemotional, matter-of-fact, almost cold tone. Ideals were back in style; but they were to be highly controlled ideals, calculated to survive the Russians, Congress, public opinion, and man himself. They were to be unideological ideals, pointed to solving specific problems. For generations, American reformers had tried to save the world. The Kennedy group appeared sure that, if the world was to be saved, it would be saved by their becoming masters of the ad hoc.

Jackie Kennedy, who long ago wearied of being asked what kind of a man Jack really is, eventually found a phrase that satisfied her. Her husband, she likes to say, is "an idealist without illusions." The President himself has done his own filling out of this somewhat enigmatic description. His foreign and domestic policies, he declared, "are the result of a rule of reason." Was he a "liberal"? an interviewer pressed him. "The common definition of a liberal today is an ideological response to every situation, whether it fits reason or not. I don't have an automatic commitment. . . If the rule of reason happens to bring you to the position that happens to be the liberal position, it is the one you have to take, but not just because it is liberal. . .." But didn't his program sound like more New Dealism? "It is reasonable to say that we've got to do something about low-income housing, we've got to do something about minimum wages, we've got to do something about our schools. Reason tells me we've got to do these things."

The crisscross of attitudes, the combination of coolness and reformism, is there wherever one touches the Administration. It is in lanky, reserved Theodore C. Sorensen, thirty-three, University of Nebraska Phi Bete, Law School honors graduate, so close to the President for so long that reporters say, "When Jack is wounded, Ted bleeds," and so much the new type that newsmen use for him combinations of adjectives such as "tough" and "sensitive," "cold" and "kindly," "ruthless" and "selfless." Almost any group of top Kennedy men presents a similar picture. On the face of it there seems little in common between Special Assistant to the President for National Security Affairs, the slim, high-strung patrician McGeorge Bundy, Republican, friend and biographer of Henry Stimson, Dean of the Faculty of Arts and Sciences at Harvard; Appointments Secretary to the President, ramrod, tight-lipped Kenneth

O'Donnell, son of a football coach, much-decorated World War II pilot, captain of the football team, then full-time in Democratic affairs; and Robert S. McNamara, a pleasant-faced, snub-nosed, non-political type, who rocketed from a shoe merchant's home background to become president of the Ford Motor Company at the age of forty-one. But before long, observers were noting a strong similarity between the men. All have hair-trigger minds; all are born managers; all have, tucked away in their heads, a dream of a better world—and wince if anybody mentions it.

Bundy represents the three in his impatience when people question him about the "ideology," the "larger trend" of the Administration. "We are meeting," he says in his clipped way, "day-by-day problems." As for toughness geared to high purpose, Sorensen caught the common assumption when he said of O'Donnell: "He knows better than most people that policy and politics are indivisible—and that it is our job to preserve the point of union between the two."

As THE Kennedy Administration entered its third month, a veteran Republican Senator sat musing about it. "I watch these boys, study them up and down —they fascinate me," the Senator remarked to a friend. "But for the life of me I can't figure out whether they are going to be a bust or a big success. I can't even figure how they fit into the long pull of things down here."

The long pull of things was clear enough. The years of F.D.R. were the watershed, taking the United States out of the nineteenth into the twentieth century, inaugurating the welfare state and fully launching America into the world. The Truman years were essentially an era of codification on the domestic front and of the first serious moves to recognize the necessities of the changed world situation. The Eisenhower period was in part sheer drift, in part an era of consolidation. The sunny President, so American, so Republican, was the bridge by which millions of the most reluctant part of the public moved over to an acceptance of the welfare state at home and of coexistence abroad.

Still clearer was the conception which the Kennedy group had of its own role. America, they were sure, had enough of codification, of consolidation, and of the wheedling of men into the twentieth century. Candidate Kennedy said it in his campaign; President Kennedy declared it in his addresses; the very restlessness of his advisers spoke it. It was high time for bold, innovating actions in both the domestic and foreign areas.

There was, however, a difficulty—and one big enough to give pause to more than Republican Senators. Though the voters elected John Kennedy President of the United States, they proceeded to give no particularly persuasive indications that they shared his mood. In the opening months of the Administration, poll after poll, editorial after editorial, straw-in-the-wind after straw-in-the-wind bespoke an America with a sodden resistance to being bothered. During previous decades, the American people, in the mysterious ways of the democratic process, had usually found their way to a President who reflected their temper—a Franklin Roosevelt for years of fear and turmoil, a Harry Truman for a mood of prickly transition, a Dwight Eisenhower for an old-shoes settling down. This time, had the American people, through the closeness of the vote, perhaps through the confusions created by strong religious divisions, put into office an Administration so far removed from the public temper that inevitably the Administration would be stymied?

Kennedy and his aides were perfectly well aware of all this. They knew the mood of the country—and that the mood of the country would be the mood of Congress. The President-elect abandoned any strategy of a hundred or of ninety days before he entered the White House. Apparently the early months were to be treated as the period of the laundry list. The Administration would try to push through Congress certain measures—most importantly, anti-recession bills, depressed-areas legislation, medical care for the aged, and federal aid to education—to which Kennedy had committed himself during the campaign and for which the need seemed pressing. A strong attempt would be made to get off to a fresh start the arms-control negotiations with the Soviet Union, American defense planning, the foreign aid program, and general U.S. relations with other nations. Meanwhile the big, the basic effort would be on.

President John Kennedy would use all the enormous educational powers of his office, would use everything—his driving intellect, the folders on the Congressmen, his million-dollar TV manner, Secretary Goldberg's strength in the workingmen's bars and Jackie Kennedy's *haute couture*, McGeorge Bundy and Dean Rusk, Caroline and the professors and Soapy Williams' inspired bloopers—President Kennedy would use everything in an all-out effort to change the mood of the country and of Congress. By 1962, so the hope seemed to run, the temper would be altered sufficiently to permit the opening of an era of genuine innovation.

Will such a strategy work? Some knowledgeable observers have their doubts. They maintain that the essence of successful leadership in a democracy is emo-

tional fire, transferring a sense of exciting commitment to the general public, and that this quality is precisely what is lacking in the gifted, hard-nosed young men of the New Frontier. The point has worried sympathetic commentators since the days when Kennedy first became a serious candidate for the Presidency and his highly favorable biographer, James MacGregor Burns, wrote that Kennedy would undoubtedly bring to the White House "bravery and wisdom; whether he would bring passion and power would depend on his making a commitment not only of mind, but of heart, that until now he has never been required to make." It kept on bothering friendly observers throughout the infinitely calculated primary and Presidential campaigns, the assembling of the no-nonsense Post-Liberals in Washington, and the first carefully burnished days of the Administration.

Along with others, the pro-Kennedy columnist Doris Fleeson warned: "Efficiently, almost coldly, President-elect Kennedy and his new team of intellectuals, investment bankers, management experts and bright young men are taking over their Washington assignments. But it is already clear that a fascinating and power-laden quality is sadly lacking—and that is personal fervor, with all that it means in warmth, excitement and flair. . . . The art or trick of leadership is not just rational action, but articulation of it in ways that reach the public's heart as well as mind. Kennedy seems almost to have set for himself the Talleyrand motto: 'Above all, no zeal.' "

When the Easter Congressional recess came and the Representatives and Senators went home to sound out their constituents, the worriers worried still more. Almost unanimously the Congressmen reported back that John Kennedy was quite popular personally but that he seemed to be generating little or no additional support for his attitudes or his specific proposals. Pro-Kennedy leaders, the New York *Times* noted, were concerned about "the President's failure to fire the general public with enthusiasm for his legislative program."

Yet there were countersigns. However slowly, the Administration bills *were* moving through Congress—and at a faster rate than during the opening months of the Eisenhower Administration. When Kennedy stubbed his toe on Cuba and came out of the experience declaring that America needed a fundamental rethinking of its foreign programs, a notable surge of public opinion agreed with him. All the while the Peace Corps, the most offbeat of the Administration proposals, continued to provoke a response that surprised even its enthusiasts. "This President," said one college president, "has touched something in the oncoming generation that the young people themselves did not realize was in them."

It could be that there was a Post-Liberal America as well as Post-Liberal leaders. It could be that this America knew, in its heart of hearts, that things should change and was gradually, warily, responding to men who managed to say so without arousing that supreme fear of the 1960s, the fear of fervor.

The President meets the press and the television cameras in the new State Department auditorium. On the platform with him are Press Secretary Pierre Salinger and his deputy, Andrew Hatcher.

President Kennedy crosses an office on his way to the Cabinet Room.

TOP, *Presidential advisers and Cabinet members chat informally before the official Cabinet meeting begins. In the foreground, Secretary of Labor Arthur Goldberg makes a point in talking with Secretary of the Interior Stewart Udall. In the background, Economic Adviser Walter Heller, Vice President Lyndon Johnson, and, with his back to the camera (facing Secretary of Commerce Luther Hodges), Secretary of Defense Robert McNamara.* CENTER, *the friendly hand is Udall's; the shoulder belongs to Attorney General Robert Kennedy.* RIGHT, *before the meeting, Secretary McNamara studies task-force reports that will be discussed.*

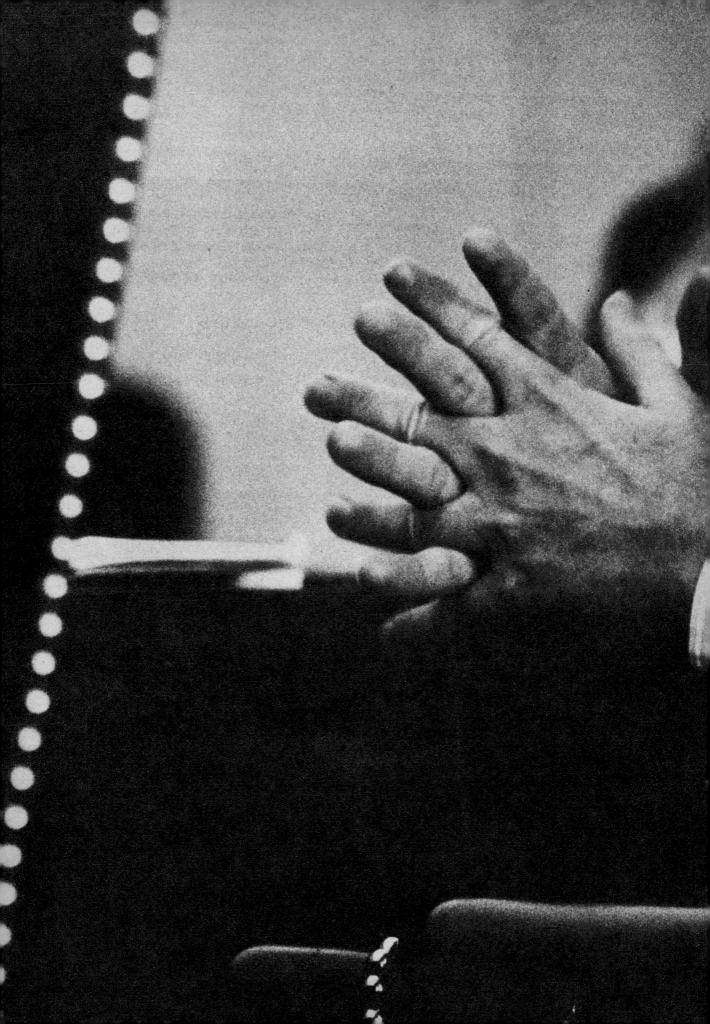

President Kennedy stops to talk with Secretary of State Rusk and visiting German officials.

The President, who cares about art and ships, comments on a choice made by his artist friend William Walton. Mr. Kennedy agreed that the picture should hang where Walton is holding it.

ABOVE, *the subject is serious: the President is being briefed by Secretary of the Treasury Dillon and other advisers prior to the meeting with German Foreign Minister Von Brentano—but there are light moments.* BELOW, *Kenneth O'Donnell, the President's Appointments Secretary, executive assistant and trouble-shooter, in his office.*

ABOVE, *Larry O'Brien, President Kennedy's "Congressional liaison man," personifies the informality of the new generation in Washington. Late in the evening he is discussing the problem of finding "the right man for the job" with his* aide, *Dick Donohue.* BELOW, *Secretary Goldberg and the President's Special Counsel, Ted Sorensen, in a whispered exchange during a meeting. On the wall is a painting depicting the PT boat adventure of the President's Navy days.*

On The Hill, Larry O'Brien makes a note, lending a sympathetic ear to a Congressman who has something political on his mind

ABOVE, *The youngest Senator, Frank Church of Idaho (keynoter at the Democratic Convention in 1960), makes an emphatic point in a discussion with the oldest Senator, Carl Hayden of Arizona.* BELOW, *Democratic Senators and Congressmen assemble in the old Supreme Court chamber for a luncheon in honor of the new Democratic Party Chairman, John M. Bailey. From left to right, Larry O'Brien, Speaker Sam Rayburn, Vice President Johnson, Representative John McCormack, Chairman Bailey and Senator Dodd of Connecticut. (The painting shows the meeting of President Lincoln's Cabinet on July 22, 1862, when the President first read the Emancipation Proclamation.)*

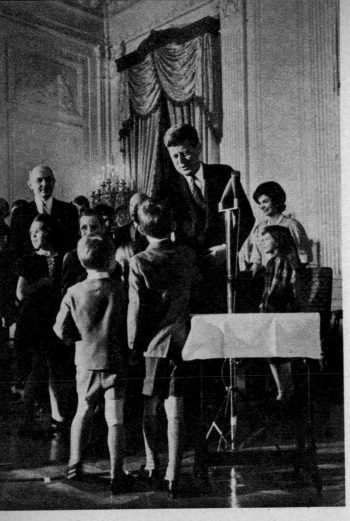

LEFT, *the President greets some of the children (including a few Kennedy nieces and nephews) who attended the swearing-in of the Cabinet.*

BELOW, *President Kennedy and the First Lady in a reception line at the White House*

"Can we forge...a grand and global alliance, north and south, east and west, that can assure a more fruitful life for all mankind?"

THE WORLD'S NEW FRONTIERS

By BARBARA WARD / Photographed by INGE MORATH

EVERY incoming American Administration plunges at once into international crisis. Ever since the nations of the North Atlantic set the world moving on the revolutionary track of political equality and capital accumulation, violent change and hence crisis have become the natural environment of man. The lulls are perfectly illusory. Underneath, the fact of crisis remains.

But if the general predicament of President Kennedy's Administration is habitual, its scale and intensity are surely new. There are signs that each of the broad political areas into which our world is divided—the North Atlantic arena, the Communist bloc, the uncommitted nations—has reached a point in its development at which major changes of direction must be expected and, in some cases, are desperately needed. Problems have been gathering momentum over the last decade. All too many now seem to be set on collision course. It seems clear that only the liveliest, most farsighted statesmanship can keep the turbulent 1960s from disaster.

THE MOOD of crisis in the uncommitted world springs from the fact that, broadly speaking, the easy stage of winding up the colonial system is now complete. After a century of confused government and patchy economic development, Latin America has come of age. Asia, apart from pockets of territory such as Goa, is free. In Africa, the settler problem—in Algeria, Kenya and the Rhodesias—still inhibits the full transfer of power from the metropolitan government to local leaders. South Africa turns its back on the future. Yet the course is clear. Africa, for good or evil, will also rule itself.

But now, what next? All through these continents rumors of a better life have spread among the people. The Andean tin miner, the cocoa grower of Ashanti, fishermen at Trivandrum, rice farmers round Dacca—all have felt in the last ten years some brush from the wings of hope, some first groping response to the revolutionary hope that tomorrow may be better than today. But the chance is, in many areas, that it will be worse.

The fine fervor of struggling together for independence fades, leaving political leaders to face the reality of divided loyalties and divided interests. In many states in Africa the frontiers themselves are arbitrary, drawn by the rivalries of France and Britain and Germany eighty or ninety years ago. Tribes may spill over their boundaries—as do the Ewes of West Africa. Their adherence to the new states may be far less rooted than their absorption in their old tribe. So far, the fissiparation of the Congo is unique, but the pressures it represents are not. A number of the new states seem to tremble on the edge of dissolution.

Even where, as in India, administration remains competent and the leaders continue to command nationwide support, the fundamental dilemma of the post-independence phase cannot be avoided. It is quite simply that economic elbowroom must be increased and the processes of growth set firmly in motion before popular revulsion sweeps away leaders who cannot "deliver." The only hope of containing tribal or linguistic difficulties and of restraining the class struggle lies in an upward swing of hope and opportunity, of literacy and employment. All this requires capital—massive capital. Yet capital is the scarcest commodity in any community in which half the people may not yet have entered the market economy at all and the other half subsist on per capita incomes of below $100 a year. Capital is saving. But who wants to save on $60 a year?

These generalizations do not cover all the developing nations. Latin America is in a special category since its independence from colonial rule is a century old and at least some of its states—Brazil, for instance, or Mexico—are well on toward achieving a developed economy. Yet the malaise of frustrated hope afflicts Latin America just the same. In the Andean republics, the mass of the people still live in the unrelieved misery of the unprogressive semi-feudal countryside; even in the more developed states, the accumulation of capital wealth by a business élite has not yet led to a wide sharing of its benefits with the people at large. In fact, economies such as Mexico's, where a very considerable momentum of growth has been achieved by vigorous enterprise and very high profits, have reached a point at which a further expansion of the industrial system can hardly be looked for unless higher wages and more purchasing power widen the domestic market.

Paradoxically, the anti-imperialist mood of other continents can also be found below the Rio Grande. One of Lenin's masterstrokes of misinterpretation was to link all forms of foreign investment with the risk of imperial control. He argued that Western investors, driven to look abroad for profits by the failure of local markets

Ambassador Adlai Stevenson at the UN General Assembly with some of his advisers

35

to expand, would secure control of foreign fields of investment and work to keep rival competitors out, either by direct imperialist intervention or by manipulating local puppet governments. In some instances the Leninist analysis was not too wide of the mark. Western intervention in China and parts of Africa had elements of this compulsion. And in some parts of Latin America the predominance of United States investment lent some force to the criticism that local governments—in Cuba, in the "banana republics"—were profoundly influenced by United States interests and pressures.

It is the misfortune of the world that Marx and Lenin should both have extrapolated into the future trends which reversed themselves almost as they wrote. Marx's "permanent impoverishment of the workers" ends as soon as the modern technological, capitalist society is in running order and its benefits, by way of higher wages, trade-union organization, the democratic vote, social security and so forth, begin to spread to the people at large—a stage which started in Britain in the 1870s and which, after many vicissitudes, may be said to have spread to the whole Atlantic world after the Second World War.

Equally Lenin's definition of imperialism always had a fatal flaw—the fact that the bulk of Western capital did not go to colonial or semi-colonial territories. At least 70 per cent of it flowed back and forth between the wealthy temperate lands—mainly around the Atlantic—of European settlement. But it became progressively more out of date as the West itself turned its back on imperialism with such changed policies as Franklin Roosevelt's "Good Neighbor" policy and the postwar liquidation of virtually the whole of the European colonial system.

But the essence of Communism today is never to allow fact to catch up with its resounding fictions. The language of the faithful still interprets Western policy in terms of exploitation and imperialism. And since in the developing world the majority are still very poor and memories of recent colonial or semi-colonial control still strong, the anti-Western slogans have their appeal. In Cuba, for instance, Castro interprets his revolution as the uprising of the masses against Batista's "puppet government" manipulated by the American "monopolies and trusts." The essence of Castroism is to carry this version of violent upheaval throughout Latin America wherever poverty, hope, frustration, entrenched privilege and foreign investment can be twisted to fit the Marxist pattern.

SUCH IS the precarious world which faces President Kennedy and his Western allies at the beginning of his Administration. The forces of instability are growing in the post-colonial areas just as Communism acquires new power and new confidence to exploit that instability. A whole world order more or less responsive to Western leadership has vanished into the limbo of history. And now the issue hangs in the balance whether the new order may not be twisted into such patterns of anti-Western hostility as underlie Castro's mouthings

of defiance and hate. For Westerners, used to a world which they more or less dominate, the shock of change is traumatic. Gone are the days of easy pre-eminence. They have to rally their wits and their fortitude and their staying power even to maintain what they have. And they must do so at a time when, even within their own community, there are signs of uncertainty and strain.

In general, the Atlantic alliance does not look in too poor a shape. Thanks very largely to the Marshall Plan, its basic economic strength is more commanding than at any previous time. Most of its members have passed across the second great threshold of economic change— the threshold of mass consumption—and all around, the North Atlantic people enjoy higher living standards and the chance of a fuller life than any group of nations in human history. More than this, they have taken some crucial steps to avoid the traps of selfish nationalism and restrictive economics which caught them fast in the two dreary decades between the world wars. The old colonial system has been more or less gracefully and more or less completely liquidated. A movement toward European unity is under way. America has behaved with unparalleled generosity, rebuilding and re-equipping nations which were bound to be not only its most effective customers but also its most effective competitors as well. Above all, the group has reversed the old historic fatality by which no democracy ever takes care of its basic security in times of supposed peace. Since 1949 the North Atlantic Treaty has bound America to Europe in an alliance which, had it been created earlier, might have deterred Hitler's aggressions.

Yet the signs of strain are unmistakable. Britain and France have reached the final stage in transforming their old empires into new associations based on friendship and common interests; but both at this stage have encountered the daunting problem of persuading minorities of their own stock, living in Africa, to accept the transfer of power to the local indigenous majorities. The Rhodesian crisis has not undermined political stability in Britain—in spite of the attacks of right-wing conservatives—but in France the poison of the long Algerian war has infected the whole political system, and although one may hope that President de Gaulle can achieve a negotiated settlement, his countervailing insistence on French nationalism, French grandeur and French independence has led to policies which weaken the NATO structure and undermine the effectiveness of the United Nations—one of the few instruments of action acceptable to the majority of the emergent nations.

French intransigence and British hesitations have also led to an economic split in Europe. . . . One consequence could be a fatal weakening of the Atlantic area's hesitant movements toward greater economic unity and freer trade.

And the problem of the American balance of payments has been intensified. Dollars and to a lesser extent sterling are used as substitutes for gold in financing the ups and downs of world trade. But international trade is expanding more rapidly than either gold or the supply of standby currencies. It runs into recurrent periods of pressure when the settlement of outstanding debt threatens to deplete reserves—rather as in Victorian times a sudden panic might lead to a run on a local bank. In those days, banks were not co-ordinated through a Federal Reserve System and the panic could lead to bankruptcy not because of any basic weakness but because sufficient liquid (or instantly available) reserves were not forthcoming. Today, the national monetary systems of the Atlantic world still have to behave as did separate banks in the nineteenth century. They have no adequate Federal Reserve System to tide them over the international moments of pressure or panic. The International Monetary Fund could in theory act in this sense, but so far its resources too are still inadequate. Thus world trade expanding beyond the scale of present reserves exposes each standby currency to the kind of pressures Britain experiences every few years and America underwent in the late summer of 1960.

But of course the chief reason for the pressure on the dollar has been America's generous readiness to shoulder the major part of the bill for economic assistance and for Western defense. The disproportion began, reasonably enough, when Western Europe was flattened by war and the United States alone had economic elbow-room. But it has been carried on by casualness and habit down to the present day when Western Europe is in fact economically more lively than some sections of American business, when Germany is accumulating foreign reserves at unparalleled speed and when the whole group of West European nations have reached a degree of adherence no one foresaw even ten years ago.

In such conditions it would seem axiomatic that they should increase their contribution both to economic assistance and to Western defense. But the axiom is not so easily accepted. Each can produce figures to show they are "doing their share" in providing assistance. The latest report from the Organization for European Economic Cooperation (OEEC) gives a breakdown of capital going overseas from Europe which suggests that most of the member nations are exporting nearly 1 per cent of their national income. But the figures are to some degree irrelevant. The estimates include the transfer of capital to wealthy areas such as Australia. Germany counts as aid such purely business arrangements as commercial credits for five years at 8 per cent. A large part of the OEEC estimate is thus not assistance at all but profitable investment.

Similarly, while lip service may be paid to the need to strengthen the NATO shield, General de Gaulle has gone far to dismantle it by removing French units from its command and by insisting on an independent French nuclear force. Britain in its turn has ended conscription and faces a rising and possibly dangerous tide of neutralist protest from the Left. Neither approach seems precisely calculated either to give NATO more force or to lessen the economic load on the United States.

SUCH IS the profile of the age of crisis which the new Administration has inherited. None of these difficulties and dangers can be bypassed or shirked, for, of their innate tendency, they are all likely to grow worse. Communism will not abandon its goal of world dominion, and the resources to back the goal will certainly increase. Developing economies cannot quickly make the transition to self-sustaining growth. Meanwhile, popular hopes—and the growth of population—must steadily increase pressure for drastic change. And in the Atlantic arena, resurgent nationalism and contradictory economics point, unless corrected, to a disintegration of the West's frail alliance and a return to the economic anarchy that marked the interwar years. Inevitably, too, a worsening of conditions on each of the three fronts deepens the crises elsewhere. A disunited NATO cannot counter Communism's growing confidence. Incoherence in the Western economies inhibits progressive, sustained economic policies to assist world development. But without such policies, developing economies will be thrust back even more tragically on their own unresolved dilemmas—and who will profit from this save the Communists? The vicious circle of interlocking crises must be broken. But how is it to be done?

It is difficult to establish priorities. The circle has to be broken at many points at once, and it is supremely fortunate for the free world that at this moment of peril the new American Administration gives the impression of commanding sufficient intellectual vigor and physical and moral energy to confront so herculean a task. The chief aim in the Atlantic world must surely be to create a community in depth, a community linked by so many indissoluble economic, social and moral links that its common life becomes the shaping influence of every national leader's politics.

One senses that both President Kennedy and Mr. Macmillan have felt their way gingerly around the problem. The published communiqués speak only in most general terms of "the need for Atlantic unity." But we may believe that in private discussions the Western leaders are striking out more ambitiously toward the West's new frontiers. A concrete first step would be a British decision to end its hesitations and join the Common Market, bringing with it, if possible, its associates in the "Outer Seven," and negotiating with it at the same time appropriate forms of association between Europe and other members of the British Commonwealth. The task should not be insuperable since an assured share in a growing European market of 200 million souls is ultimately more attractive than preferences in a static British market a fourth that size. Moreover, as European industry sweeps forward, old-fashioned high-cost peasant farming in Western Europe will give way to more modern and competitive techniques and lessen the need for Europe's present high levels of agricultural protection. Here, perhaps, is the first and most urgent task for America's new President—to encourage Mr. Macmillan to take the plunge and to persuade de Gaulle to let him do so.

A second step would lie in persuading Britain to take the lead in restoring sufficient military strength to the NATO alliance—including conventional strength—an issue over which the West European allies have always lagged, and never more severely than now.

But these are only first steps. Adding Britain to Europe and increasing Europe's military establishment could conceivably encourage the revival of the "Third Force" philosophy in which Europe acts as an independent broker and buffer state between America and Russia. Such a policy is totally unrealistic. The world does not need any more blocs and counterblocs. It needs one steadily widening area of economic co-operation and settled freedom. And, ideals apart, only with American might added to European strength can the West maintain that *overplus* of power on the side of freedom which makes the pursuit of an East-West balance of power in any way secure.

Some of those policies are already above the horizon of discussion—a new Atlantic Federal Reserve System or an extension of the International Monetary Fund to take the strain off the dollar and to ensure that enough liquid reserves underpin a steady expansion of world trade, the negotiation of a low tariff or no-tariff agreement which by stages, say, over the next twenty-five years, brought North America into a new free trade relationship with Europe, a Development Bank with the especial function of speeding funds to any areas crippled by the onslaught of new competition. Such funds have re-equipped depressed areas in Europe—one thinks of the Borinage in Belgium. Similar investment has tided Lancashire over its dependence upon textiles to a point at which it has become a major engineering region—and India's exports of cheap textiles to Britain have steadily increased.

And to such economic steps in the process of "getting mixed up together"—to use Sir Winston Churchill's homely phrase—one should add social and political action on the lines prefigured in Europe—reconciliation of social-security schemes and salary scales, approximations of legal codes, interchange of academic degrees and professional qualifications, some increase in mobility for men as well as capital, joint experiments in education, consultative political machinery.

Such an enlargement of scale and opportunity would do more than create an organization capable of withstanding the steady advance of Communist power. It would send a new breath of vitality and action stirring right through the Atlantic world. It is no coincidence that since the formation of the Common Market in 1958 hitherto stagnant economies such as France's have undergone a remarkable spurt of growth, that rates of expansion inside the Common Market have reached levels of 6 and 7 per cent a year—probably higher than Soviet rates—and that a technological widening and transformation of the old narrow class markets of Western Europe has created a newer, gayer world where artistry and resource create exciting new patterns in exports and industrial design. The change has more than economic consequences. Below the level of Europe's present aging leaders a new generation presses forward, better trained, better educated, less concerned with the parochialisms of the past, more ready for new challenge and adventure.

SUCH AN economy would also be in a proper posture to sustain the long task of underpinning, economically, socially, politically, the post-colonial world. It is above all in this field that the first months of the Kennedy Administration have shown a new imaginative perception of the policies involved. The President and his officers have ranged themselves squarely with anti-colonial sentiment and tactfully but firmly underlined their conviction that Europe can never create a new relationship with the emerging continents if it clings to old discredited patterns of overlordship. They have shown sympathetic understanding of the complex motives behind neutralism. They are attempting to preserve the United Nations as an instrument for dealing impartially with post-colonial turmoil of the Congo stamp. All this has created in the developing states a revival of friendly feeling toward America, especially in the critical forum of the United Nations, where, only last fall, a seismic shift of world opinion toward Soviet attitudes appeared to be under way.

They have also proposed four crucial changes in the direction and administration of economic assistance. They are pledged to secure matching contributions from their European allies. The percentage discussed—1 per cent of national income—should secure a flow of Western aid of some eight billion dollars, probably two or three billion more than is available today. Moreover, by increasing greatly the contributions of countries such as Germany which are running a large and steady surplus on their foreign-trade account, it would directly reduce the strain on the American balance of payments.

In the second place, the Administration is aware that the rhythms of development are not those of annual budgetary appropriations. In spite of the supposed check on spending induced by Congressional control, the annual method may even be more wasteful, since no scheme can be considered over its proper period of gestation; and there is even an inducement to spend money in a haphazard way toward the end of the financial year since there is no necessary carry-over of commitments to the next season. Yet a developing economy needs a decade and more to see it through the "big push" of original investment, and it is some such period of time that the Administration has in mind when it asks for lending powers independent of annual Congressional approval and control.

The third important innovation lies in the Administration's insistence upon a serious strategy for development. Economies do not acquire momentum and powers of sustained expansion simply by the chance expenditure of large sums of money. Expensive barracks, luxury yachts, public palaces, monster administrative offices eat up funds and show nothing in return. Only if capital is dedicated carefully to education, to "infrastructure"—power, ports, transportation—to the modernizing of agriculture, to suitable industrial expansion, does the beneficent cycle of growth sparking more growth begin. Some economies are not yet in a condition to devise such a strategy. For them, a "pre-investment" program is needed—to survey resources, get education started and devise a pattern of growth. At the other end of the spectrum, countries like India—or Brazil or Mexico—have reached a stage where a massive injection of capital in the next ten years will probably bring about the momentum needed for self-sustaining expansion. An aid program must be flexible enough to meet all these different needs. It must be sufficiently co-ordinated to avoid waste and overlapping. And, above all, it must be sustained.

The last and perhaps the most important change of direction proposed by the new Administration concerns the social implications of development. There are certain forms of social structure which make the growth of a modern economy virtually impossible. Not only do they inhibit growth as such; they make certain that even if growth occurs the people in general will not share in it. An unreformed feudal oligarchy neither develops its own resources nor permits its tenants to do the job instead. A business class bent on real estate and housing gains and "conspicuous waste" in all its forms will not provide sufficient impetus for general investment. When, therefore, in his program for Latin America, the President puts wholly new emphasis upon reforms in land tenure and in the tax system to ensure that effort is fairly rewarded and productive capital fully encouraged, he does more than lay down ground rules for economic success. He begins to counter Communism in an area where hitherto it has found its most effective targets—among the selfish, irresponsible, self-regarding elite of old landlord and new entrepreneur in the developing economy. By seeking to expand literacy, train artisans, extend rapidly the managerial and professional classes, the Administration's new version of economic assistance can become an instrument of social liberation as well.

These, then, are the new directions which could give guidance and impetus to the developing economies; and since some of the greatest—the Indian subcontinent, large parts of Latin America—will reach the verge of a "take-off" to sustained growth in the 1960s, the next ten years could be a "decade of development" in the fullest sense.

One can now see why, without indulging in the rather tarnished rhetoric of anti-Communism, the programs of the new Administration begin to add up to the first genuinely effective long-term strategy for dealing with Communism that the free world has evolved since the end of the Marshall Plan. It seeks to revive the core of Atlantic strength and to give the alliance the weapons and the capabilities it needs not only for a major atomic struggle but for the Communists' chosen instrument of brush-fire wars as well. It aims at building an Atlantic economy strong, competitive and supple enough to meet the rising needs of its own people and to provide essential capital for the modernization of the emergent world. It outlines a strategy for securing this development within a social and political framework which offers some hope of justice and opportunity for everyone. Above all, it begins to produce a philosophy of Western action which can counter effectively the most powerful Communist myths.

For what is at the root of their constant, implacable, universal propaganda against the West? It is quite simply that now, as in the last three hundred years, the Western Powers are the exploiters and despoilers of the world. Their investments entail servitude. Their economic interests seek political protection and hence control. Their trade favors the developed against the underdeveloped, the rich against the poor. Their only purpose in the world at large is to enrich themselves, however much, in the process, they may impoverish the masses everywhere else.

This attitude has in it enough of past history and current fact mixed up with its falsehoods to be a dangerous brew for the aspiring and impatient peoples of the developing world. It cannot be counted simply by words and protestations. It has to be shown in actual physical fact to be blatantly untrue. A new image of the West has to efface the old picture of imperialists and exploiters. A first step—the ending of direct empire—is being taken. But the second still lies ahead. It is to replace the old image of exploitation with the new vision of an "alliance for progress," of co-operation and partnership between equal peoples to replace the old patterns of servitude and unequal power.

We know from our free domestic society how such a world must be organized. Behind the clash of arms and interests and the present uneasy balance of power, we have to seek disarmament and a world under law. This demands the co-operation of Communists whose present hostility makes immediate agreement remote. But ordered society also demands "the general welfare," and this we can pursue greatly and imaginatively whether or not the Communists co-operate. And who knows whether, after a decade or so of genuinely competitive coexistence in bringing peace and bread to the world, even the Communists may lose some of their *furor theologicus* and work with the West for the larger visions of progress and good will. We do not know. But, to quote Sir Winston Churchill once more, we need not believe that "God has despaired of His children."

THE OPPORTUNITIES await us. The new frontiers of the world are more challenging than any that have yet opened to questing man. But shall we ride out to conquer them? Has the West the courage and initiative needed to ask not what the world will do for them but what they can do for the world?

Here the doubts begin. In the last ten years, all of the Atlantic arena has entered into the satisfactions and distractions of the affluent society. The trumpets may sound from the steep but from the people comes only a muffled reply. The young leader of America, the older leaders of Europe have not yet been able to convince their fellow countrymen that the age is one of heroic opportunity and heroic risk. The verdict on the world's new frontiers must, therefore, be that it is no longer certain that Western man will be in the vanguard, no longer self-evident that he will be the pioneer. The fateful question remains whether, while gaining affluence, he may not have lost his vision and his soul.

The chairman of the U.S.S.R. delegation to the UN, Andrei Gromyko, demands the dismissal of Secretary General Dag Hammarskjöld and accuses him of the murder of Patrice Lumumba.

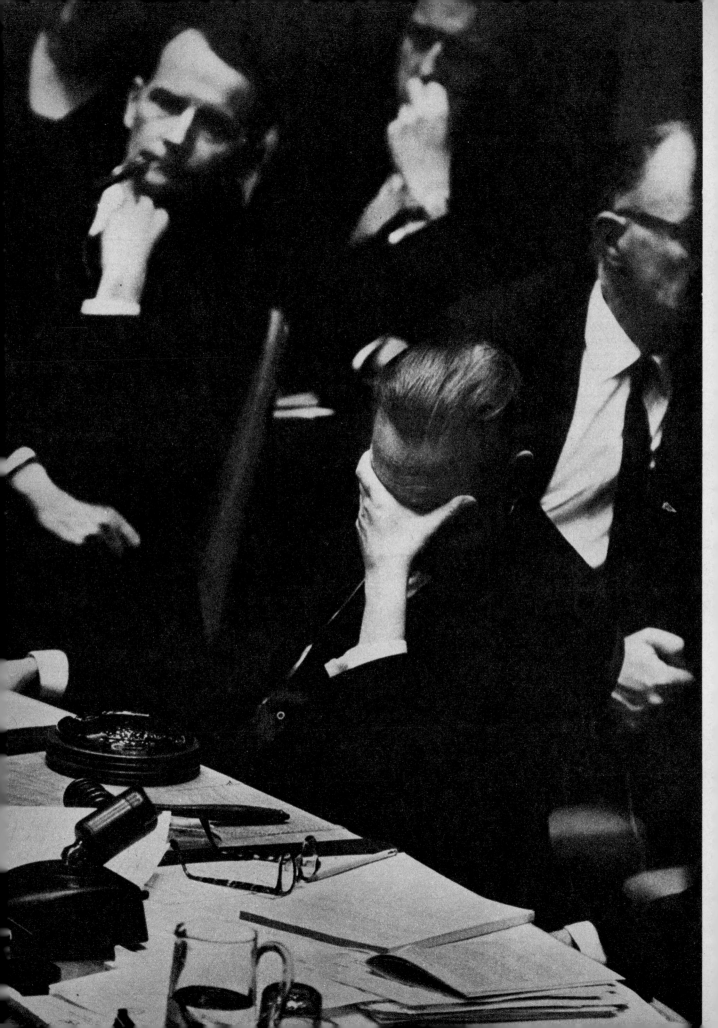

Adlai Stevenson listens to the Gromyko speech in the General Assembly and at the same time finishes his own first address to the Assembly, which was a stern reply to Russian accusations against Hammarskjöld.

OSITE

mmarskjöld listens to the debate Security Council session on the plicated African issues.

43

Ambassador Stevenson at a party given for him by the members of the delegation from Nigeria. To Stevenson's right, Nigerian Ambassador Alhaji Muhammad Ngileruma, and in the background, in national dress, the Nigerian Ambassador's wife.

RIGHT

The President and Ambassador Stevenson meet in the White House prior to Stevenson's conference with Secretary of State Dean Rusk and Foreign Minister Gromyko.

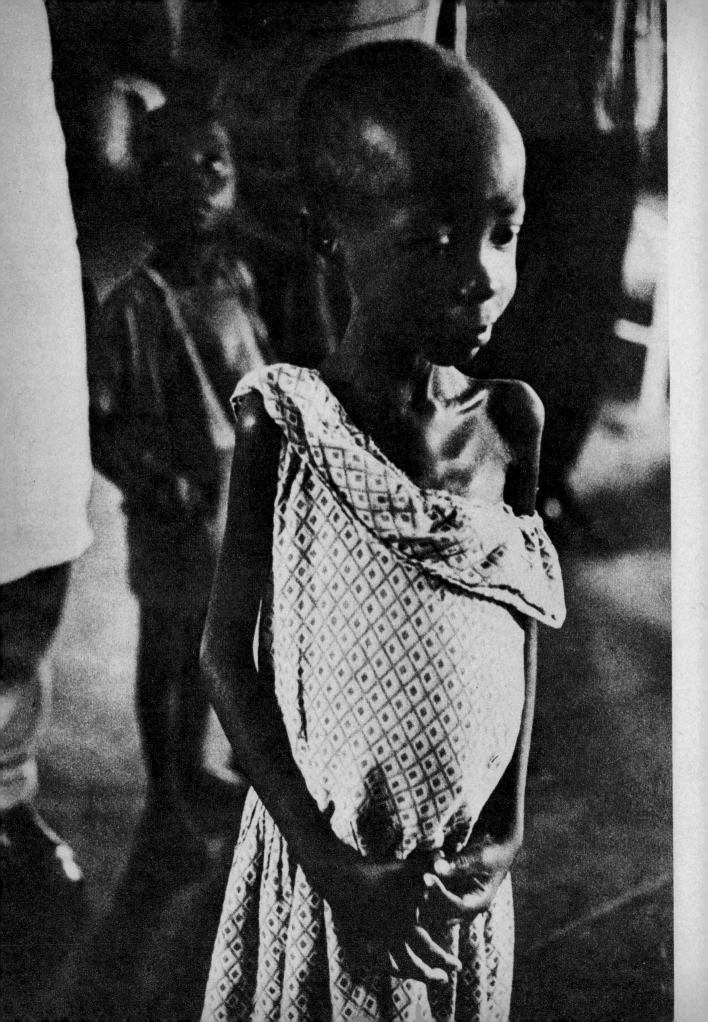

FAMINE IN THE KASAI

Text and Photographs by MARC RIBOUD

IN THE FIRST WEEK of March 1961 I am in the Congo and can see that the Africans in Leopoldville have enough to eat, for Brazzaville is nearby and communications are good.

I fly to Bakwanga, capital of the "autonomous state" of South Kasai, to watch the food distribution. The plane (a U.S. one chartered by the UN) carries an American I.C.A. team which is going to see how U.S. food is being distributed. Henry Wiens heads the team—a man typical of the new young government whose principle is to "go and see for himself." The first thing he sees when we land in Bakwanga is four Congolese, who come inside the plane to unload the bags of rice. First they pick up the few grains scattered on the floor, fold them in a handkerchief and stuff them into their pockets. This is three hours away from Leopoldville.

Every day people, mainly children, are dying of hunger.

How can famine have started in a green, hospitable, fertile region called Kasai? Last September, a centuries-old rivalry between the Lulua and Baluba, two close ethnic groups, was revived. The Balubas' home region is the South Kasai (the area around Bakwanga), but many Balubas followed the Belgians into Lulua territory. After independence and the Belgians' departure, the Balubas soon found themselves unprotected, outnumbered and caught again in their old rivalry with the Luluas. They began an exodus to the South Kasai, some of them walking great distances.

In two months, 300,000 Baluba refugees arrived in the South Kasai, whose population before this influx was one million people, all of them with food but, as everywhere in Africa, with no reserves. The chaotic political situation brought on a bad harvest, and this, coupled with the sudden increase of the population, has utterly disrupted the precarious balance—and everybody is starving.

Finally, an SOS to the world, to the UN. The airlift starts at the end of December and the first food is distributed the day before Christmas. Twenty-five planes land every day in Bakwanga airport, bringing rice, flour, milk, dried fish from all over the world. Russian sugar is mixed with American powdered milk.

In January an announcement comes from Washington. The States will send food in great amounts: 10,000 tons of cornmeal, 10,000 tons of rice, 6,000 tons of powdered milk. The fight against hunger gains momentum, the death rate goes down. Now the food starts to come in overland, which means a month's trip from the port to Kasai: by rail, by riverboat, again by rail, then by truck. Sometimes a convoy is delayed and there is no distribution.

Normally a convoy of about twenty UN trucks arrives in Bakwanga every other day. There the food is loaded onto other trucks, driven by Congolese, and taken to distribution centers all over the South Kasai. From then on no UN personnel is seen with the food. In the villages the local authorities take care of distribution. They organize a system of ration cards. Food is given by African hands into African hands, by Balubas to other Balubas.

Sometimes an inscription is seen on a bag of rice: "Gift from the U.S." But who can read?

No one knows how many thousands of people died of hunger in Kasai during the last four months, and no one knows how many thousands more would have died without UN food relief, without the flour, the rice, the milk given by the U.S. and other countries.

In January, hundreds died every day. The situation has improved. But the Balubas need no statistics to know how precarious their situation still is—that today, tomorrow and the next day so many will die of hunger, and this will be true in June, in July, in August.

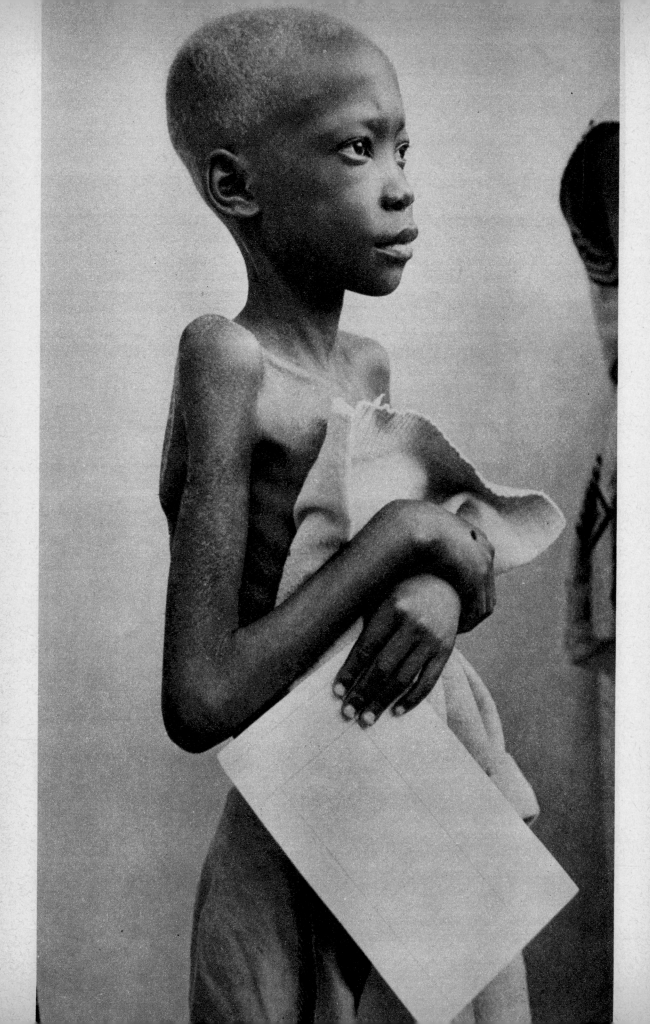

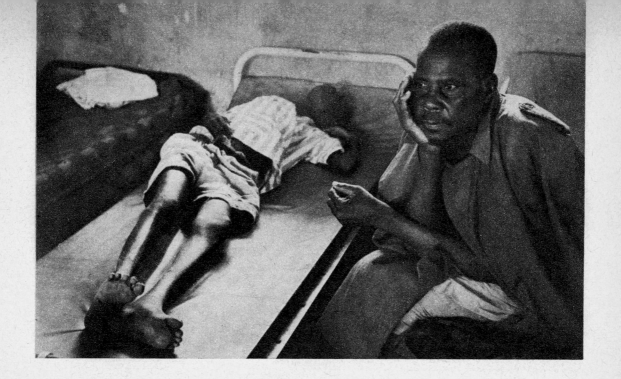

The hospital at Miabi. The children are suffering from kwarshiokor, the Ghanian name for the disease involving the lack of protein intake and resulting in malnutrition. They are waiting to be examined and given food rations.

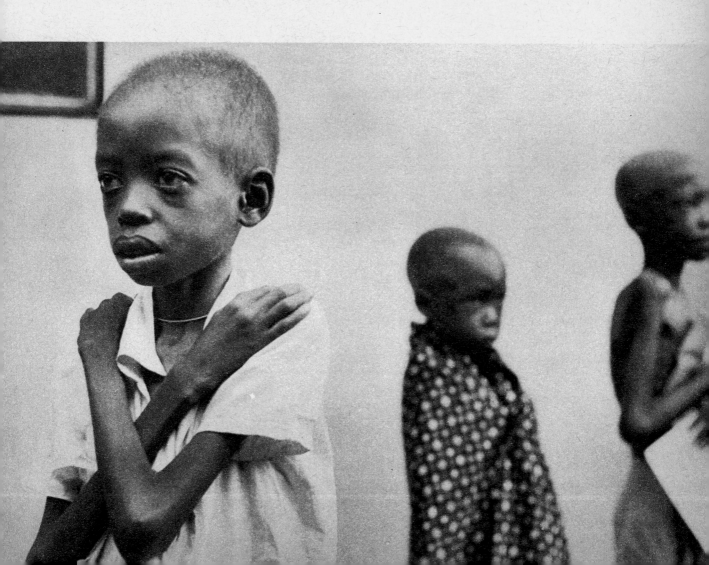

This UN convoy is bringing flour sent from the United States.

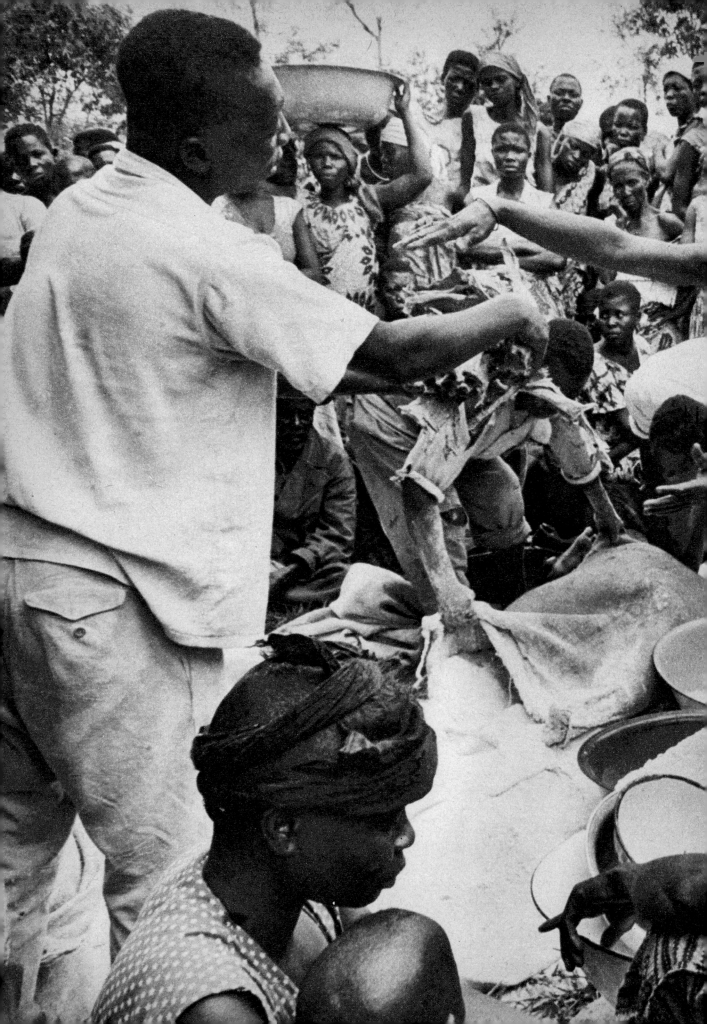

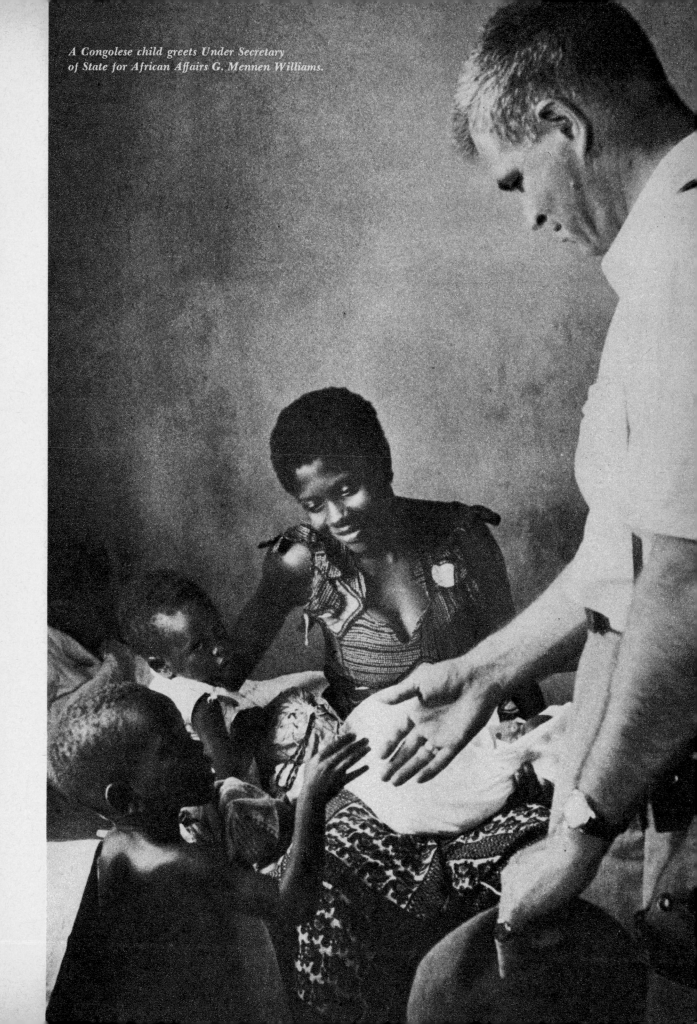

A Congolese child greets Under Secretary of State for African Affairs G. Mennen Williams.

*"To those peoples in the huts and villages of half the globe
struggling to break the bonds of mass misery.
we pledge our best efforts to help them
help themselves...."*

THE NEW WATER PUMP

Text and photographs by CONSTANTINE MANOS

SOME MILES outside the town of Riobambas in the Andes of Ecuador stands a working example of how the U.S. can help people in underdeveloped areas to help themselves. It is a water pump, a gift from the people of the United States through CARE. It cost only one hundred dollars.

In use continually, the pump serves a rural area which has never known the blessing of a steady source of pure water. Previously, drinking water had come from the same streams used for washing clothes and bathing. With it came typhus, dysentery, and all the other maladies of impure drinking water. In the dry season, water had come from mud holes, and often there was no water at all.

The new pump has brought more than water to the region, however; it has given the people a feeling of community. For the first time the inhabitants of the thatched straw huts scattered over the surrounding mountainsides have a center, a gathering place. Here the children play together, and neighbors whose huts face each other across the valleys exchange gossip.

Around the pump a village square is forming; next to it stands a new school. The local laborers who installed the pump have built over it a trestle supporting four fifty-gallon drums. From these drums the water will flow to showers being installed in the school. For the animals a drain under the pump catches the waste water and siphons it into a nearby trough.

A powdery dust pervades all in this area; it clogs the nostrils and grits on the teeth. Even in the season of rain, the pregnant clouds refuse to yield their burden. The earth is choking in its own dust, parched. Late in the afternoon one sees a line of women trudging up a steep path to their homes; on their backs are great earthenware jars filled with water from the pump. With this water they will sprinkle their small gardens and wash the dust from their faces. With this water they will prepare the meals for their families.

These women and the families they feed know little about politics. They do know that this precious water came from the new pump, which came from the United States of America.

*"But we shall always hope to find them
strongly supporting their own freedom…"*

WAR IN LAOS

Photographed by NICOLAS TIKHOMIROFF

BANGKOK: *"… and I managed to serve as a co-pilot of
an American helicopter to go pick up the wounded in an
outpost right in the middle of the jungle. The spot where
we landed is continually bombarded, and what with the
slowness of our transportation, I was not feeling very
safe.… Luckily my fright didn't show much, since the
temperature was about 110 degrees in the shade, caus-
ing one to perspire anyway.… The post is called Khu-
kacha and is about 60 miles from Louang Prabang.…
We stopped only long enough to evacuate the wounded
men (see page 66) while under constant artillery fire.…
Yet, strangely, the Laotians are basically a peace-loving
people.… The most heard Laotian phrase is 'bo pen
nyan,' meaning, roughly, 'too bad—but what can we do
about it?' … They are fond of their soft music, their
elaborate festivals…"*

"...and the American on the spot, Ivan Klecka, wh
works for the USIS [United States Information Service]
He has a wonderful beard, which impresses the Laotian
very much.... We went together three times into th

brush and to Louang Prabang. He goes to villages to put on shows for the Laotian peasants and soldiers . . . and he often must seek permission from the military personnel to let him go into some village in the forbidden zone . . . and I watched him in Bam Done, 18 miles from Louang Prabang, distributing cards, playing with children, eating with peasants, improvising a stage for the show, etc. . . ."

"...and unwilling to witness or permit the slow undoing of those human rights to which this nation has always been committed..."

CIVIL RIGHTS:

THE STRANGEST REVOLT

By WALLACE WESTFELDT, Jr.

Photographed by HENRI CARTIER-BRESSON

THE Negro in the South is in revolt.

His revolution is, indeed, the strangest in the history of the United States and certainly one of the strangest in the history of the world. And it is the essential fact of civil rights facing President Kennedy and his brother Robert.

It is a revolution in which the revolutionists bear no arms, throw up no street barricades, stone no police and, with remarkably few exceptions, initiate no violence.

It began slowly—with the first education for the Negro. It gained impetus about twenty-five years ago when Negroes started using in earnest the existing legal system to overturn existing custom and habit in the law

itself. It reached a high point on May 17, 1954, when the United States Supreme Court declared that race could not be used as a basis for determining admission to public schools.

Since May 1954, however, the tactics of the revolution have changed dramatically. Negroes in the South have become frustrated at the snail-like pace of integration in public schools, frustrated over the failure of the Congress to enact what Negroes consider necessary civil rights legislation, frustrated with the national political parties for not putting into practice what they preach at election time.

Legal action as a weapon has been shifted to the position of the siege gun. To spearhead the attack, the Negroes are relying on a strange amalgam of weapons: an awesome conviction in their cause, flanked by economic strength on the one hand, and on the other simply by their bodies, which they passively offer in resistance to the enemy.

The revolution's leadership also has shifted—from the National Association for the Advancement of Colored People and its generals of the courtroom to a loosely organized group of clergymen rather loosely led by the Reverend Martin Luther King. And the battle-cry now heard in churches throughout the South as well as at scenes of stand-ins and sit-ins is an old spiritual that says simply, "We shall overcome..."

IN Macon County, Alabama, Coahoma County, Mississippi, in Fayette County, Tennessee, and in Orleans Parish, Louisiana, Negroes persist in their efforts to send their children to white schools and to register to vote in counties where Negro voters and integrated schools in the past have been as rare as separate facilities that were equal.

■ Negroes in New Orleans, at last gaining a foot in the door of public school integration, a very tiny foothold at that, refuse to retreat from this stand despite the full political weight of the state of Louisiana being thrown against them.

■ In Atlanta, Nashville, Columbia and Rock Hill, South Carolina—and even in Mississippi—Negro students sit-in, stand-in, kneel-in and read-in at eating places, theaters, churches and libraries as they intensify their drive to eliminate racial segregation in those areas of public life that are non-governmental.

■ At Clarksville, the seat of Coahoma County, Negroes meet openly in a church to install the new president of the state branch of the NAACP. In the audience is a scattering of people from the professions, but the significant majority of the 150 persons present is representative of the Negro working class, the domestic servants and the field hands—men and women who depend on Mississippi's traditional relationships between whites and blacks for their daily bread. Their presence at the meeting, endorsing in effect a movement which assiduously plots the downfall of the Mississippi way of life as most Negroes know it, gives the meeting a grassroots aspect not generally conceded by whites to exist among Negroes in Mississippi.

■ The Fayette County Civic and Welfare League, originally created to spur the registration of Negro voters, is now placing heavy emphasis on its welfare function. Its new job: to help the Negro families evicted by white

landowners in reprisal, the Negroes say, for the act of registration. To take care of these families, the Negroes have established two tent camps—they call them Freedom Villages—which now house 150 men, women and

children. The landowners say farm mechanization, not voter registration, prompted the evictions, and they offer records of increased sales of mechanical cottonpickers in the county to support their claim. On the basis of complaints filed with the United States Department of Justice, a Federal court granted a temporary petition restraining certain landowners from further evictions. Other landowners, however, still have freedom of action, and evictions are continuing.

So is the registration of Negro voters. Where once there was only a handful of registered Negro voters, there are now close to 3,000.

■ In Macon County, the situation is similar to that in Fayette County but somewhat less severe. And the reprisal, while potentially harsh, has been more impersonal.

Confronted with a white board of registrars that has done almost everything to avoid registering Negroes—including one case where a registrar hid in a courthouse vault so Negroes could not find him—the Negroes have taken their case to court twice and threaten to do so a third time. When the state legislature gerrymandered densely populated Negro neighborhoods out of the town of Tuskegee, including the area of the famed Negro private school of Tuskegee Institute, Negroes filed suit in Federal court and the gerrymander was ultimately declared invalid. When continued efforts to register were met with continued harassment and delay, the Negroes filed complaints with the justice department of the United States Commission on Civil Rights. Suit by the Government has now been tried in Federal court, and it may well result in the first use of Federal referees in voter registration in the nation.

Now faced with the threat by the Alabama legislature

simply to abolish Macon County as a political unit, the Negroes, led by the Tuskegee Civic Association, have declared that if this act comes to pass, they will immediately challenge it in Federal court.

■ The Macon County story also shows clearly that Negroes can—and will—fight back outside the courts if pressed hard enough. When the state legislature gerrymandered Negro neighborhoods out of Tuskegee, Negroes stopped patronizing stores owned by whites. The result: white businessmen and merchants were effectively denied access to an estimated $13 million that flowed into the county from the payrolls of a Veterans Administration hospital and Tuskegee Institute. A dozen small businesses in Tuskegee, owned by white merchants, folded. Negroes set up their own businesses, including a supermarket, and today they are booming while commercial Tuskegee is nothing but a ghost of its former self.

So THE Negroes are attacking—but their weapons are peaceful methods. It is the white man's defense of his own supremacy that brings violence to the battlefield:

■ White police in Jackson break up a peaceful march of Negro students protesting the arrest of other students for attempting to break the segregation barrier in the public library. The police use tear gas, clubs and dogs to stop the march. The students say they will march again, dogs or no dogs.

■ In Columbia, a peaceful sit-in of Negro students at a drugstore lunch counter is disrupted as a white man stabs a Negro student. The next day, Negro students return to the scene of the stabbing and sit-in again.

■ In Nashville, where most of the goals being sought by Negroes elsewhere in the South have been achieved, Negro students stand-in at theaters. One night, some of them are stoned by white hoodlums. A leader of the students tells his followers, "Let every stone thrown at you be an opportunity to know yourself, your moral strength, your moral conviction in the justness of your cause." The next night the students are standing-in again.

THE REVOLUTION'S strength among Negroes is unquestioned by Negroes. It has a growing number of followers committed to it but, more important, all Negroes in the South are committed *by* it. For no Negro in his right mind dares oppose it openly.

There is no doubt there are Negroes who are disturbed by the passive-resistance technique. But they must go

along with it. One of the most influential Negro leaders in Atlanta said: "Most of us support the goals wholeheartedly but many of us may question the way they're going about it. However, we can't express this openly because if we did, the young students and the clergymen would ask us, 'Then you mean it is right for us to eat in segregated places?' Of course we don't, but by putting the whole movement on a moral plane, all open opposition has been contained."

The movement also draws strength from the growing economic power of Negroes, a fact which, ironically, means white businessmen in the cities of the South are also committed by the movement. In Atlanta, the purchasing power of Negroes is roughly estimated at over $200 million a year. It is not difficult to imagine the reaction of white merchants when Negroes use strength like this to back up the students' efforts to open up lunch counters. If a boycott is even half successful, the stores are badly hurt.

And if sit-ins or stand-ins provoke even sporadic violence from whites and unsettle the shopping area atmosphere, the trade feels it because customers of all colors stay away.

Paradoxically, much of the success of the revolution depends on the manner in which the white people of the South react to it. If they are quickly reconciled to it, all areas of public life will be integrated at a much faster pace than ever believed possible. If they fight it, they face certain economic loss with no real hope of succeeding in their fight. Richmond has fallen again and so has Atlanta, and there is no reason to believe that Birmingham or Charleston or Jackson will escape a similar fate.

Negroes in the South realize that the shift in tactics from strictly legal action to passive demonstration symbolized by the sit-in has cost them the support of some white persons who were willing to go along with them as long as the conflict was confined to the courtroom. These are persons who see little difference between the sit-ins and the segregationists' demonstrations in front of integrating public schools.

The Negroes say students in sit-ins have not once violated a community's order, and that disorder has been caused by white persons objecting to the sit-ins. They insist that to criticize the participant of the sit-in in the same breath as one criticizes the protesting segregationist is to equate one who risks a community's order to seek justice with one who violates a community's order to preserve injustice.

The new Justice Department has made it clear, through its vigorous participation in the New Orleans school case as a friend of the court, that it will act in similar fashion in other school cases. And its prosecution of voting rights cases in both Tuskegee and Fayette County strongly underscores its interest in that field. So it is clear that the new Administration is ready to aid the revolution wherever it can.

Freedom Village—the city of tents—in Fayette
County, just south of Somerville, Tennessee

Outside a general store in Brownsville, Mississippi

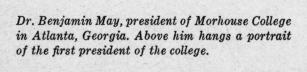
Dr. Benjamin May, president of Morhouse College in Atlanta, Georgia. Above him hangs a portrait of the first president of the college.

The audience has just marched back to the First Baptist Church in Nashville, Tennessee, after a stand-in demonstration. The Reverend James Lawson is discussing details in terms of "the next one."

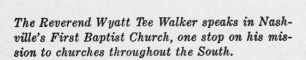

The Reverend Wyatt Tee Walker speaks in Nashville's First Baptist Church, one stop on his mission to churches throughout the South.

Saturday afternoon at a movie house in Nashville. Stand-ins and sit-ins have been successful at lunch counters and in variety stores. Now they are starting at the movie houses.

Sit-in at a drugstore in Nashville

LEFT, *a mansion typical of the opulent homes in the rich farming section of southwest Georgia. This one is in La Grange.*

Second-grade students at a public school in Nashville

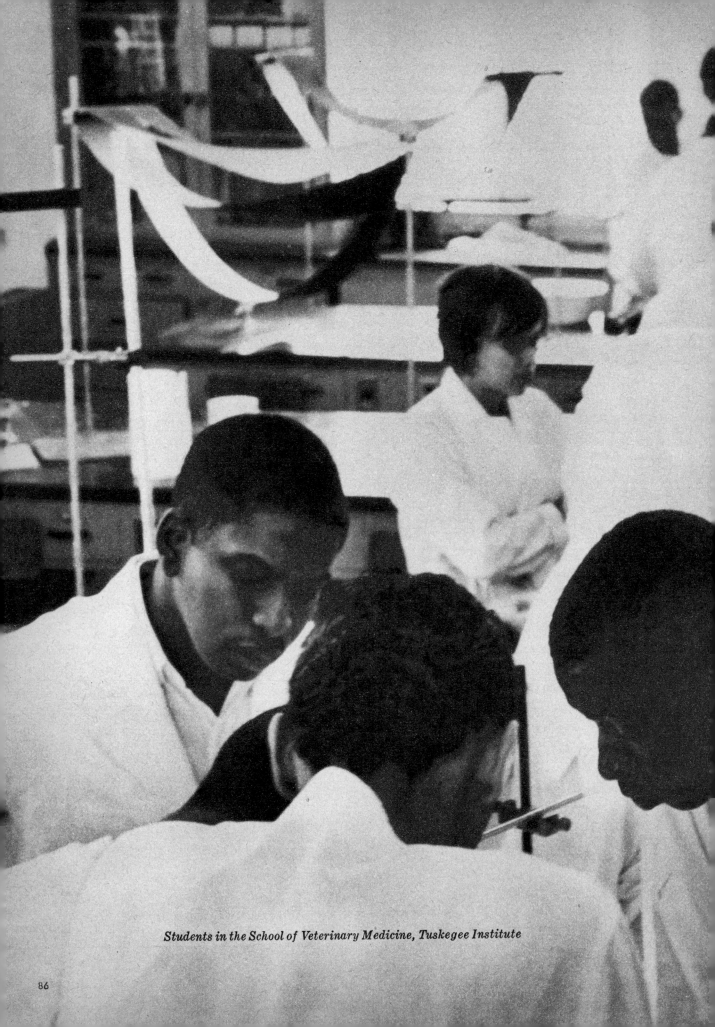

Students in the School of Veterinary Medicine, Tuskegee Institute

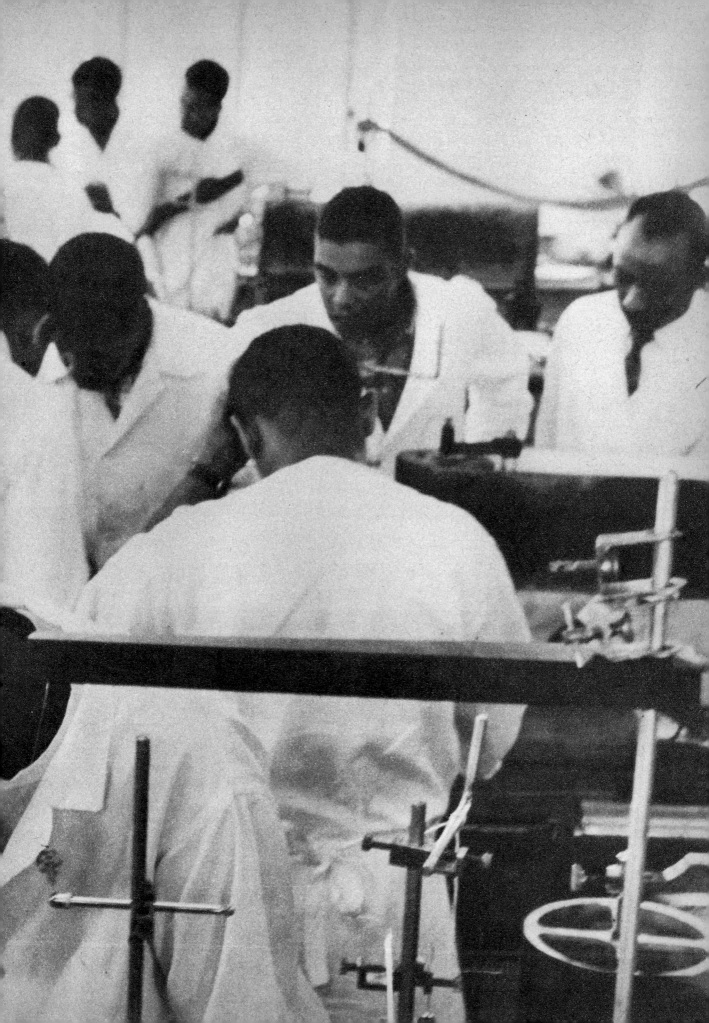

*Another installment payment
is due and collected*

*A counter at a branch of the Negro-owned
Citizens Trust Company in Atlanta*

"I look to the Lord. He promised to be a shelter. His word ain't going to fail."

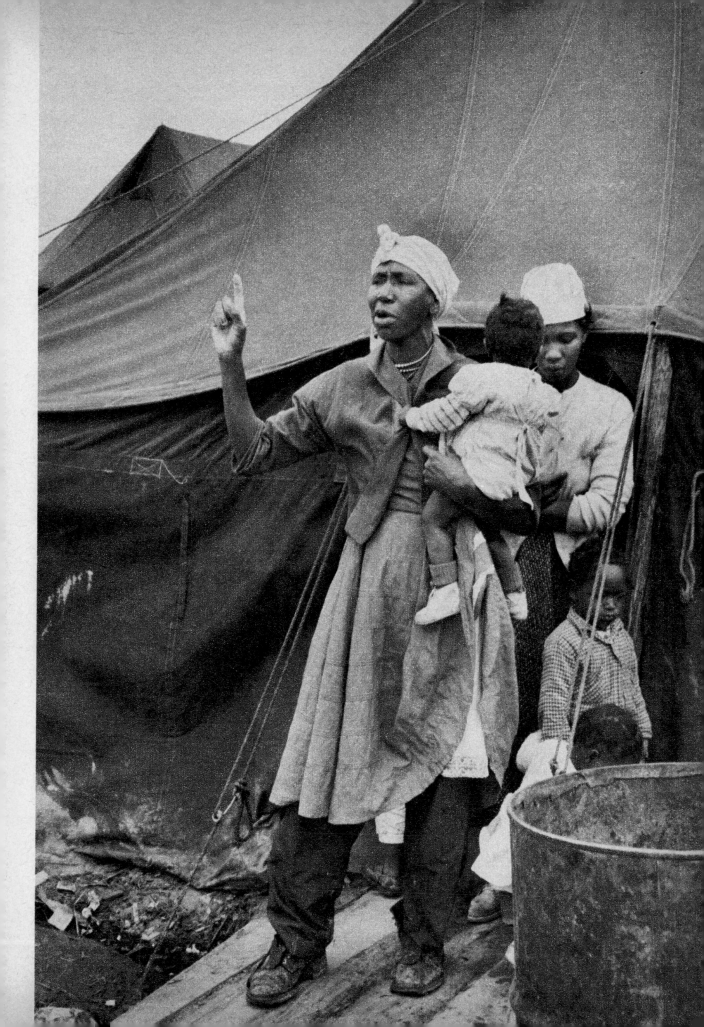

"We dare not forget that we are the heirs of that first revolution."

THE ECONOMY: WHAT GOES ON HERE?

by IRA WOLFERT / Photographed by BURT GLINN

A RECORD number of people at work and out of work.... The number of factories, mills and plants closing or going on a short week increasing steadily, while the Gross National Product rises, too—to an all-time high. ...A recession ending for everybody except the unemployed. What's going on here?

This will give you an idea: While the railroads have been staggering under agonizing body blows, a plodding plowhorse competitor they killed stone-dead and buried a century ago—barge traffic—has been reviving at such a prodigious rate that, to handle it on tracks, the railroads would have had to build one new coast-to-coast system every single year since 1947. A humdinger of a system at that, with enough rolling stock to carry three million ton miles of freight per mile of road per year.

Any human society has always been a jigsaw puzzle ever in the process of completion on a table that never stops moving. But here's a puzzle that seems to have been thrown out the window.

Pittsburgh and Detroit, the great cathedrals of American know-how to which production men from all over the world once made reverent pilgrimages, are now chronically depressed areas! Meanwhile 500 square miles of remote, sand-whipped, sun-bleached Texas prairie in the Beaumont area have been carpeted nearly wall-to-wall with brand-new factories, mills, plants, among them $400,000,000 ones, several the largest of their kind in the world. At the same time that the lines grow in front of the unemployment-compensation windows, there are more and more strenuously seductive Help Wanted ads than ever. In their hunger, big companies are even devoting $500,000 to commercials on TV networks, not to sell their products, but to entice help in making more of them.

There's a clue to all this. Seymour Wolfbein, the chief economist of the U.S. Department of Labor, puts it this way:

America made history in 1957. It was history of a kind no other nation has ever made before. For the first time in the millenniums of struggle against scarcity, a nation appeared on earth that could do it all with the left hand. From 1957 on, a steadily increasing majority of Americans have been employed in the service industries rather than in producing commodities.

"This is *the* life-giving event of the century," Dr. Wolfbein told me. How can I live? Once that was the question for every man as he came into the world. Now it's: What shall I do with my life?

This is a new situation, the result of new kinds of machines plus a new kind of social system in which they could flourish. That is what got us to this turning point in the human condition. Now the same forces are pushing us into strange country.

A nation's processes proceed—with dazing celerity—in this century. In the White House, President Eisenhower took the posture of a general reviewing a parade. President Kennedy's posture is: concern for the marchers, to put those being trampled down back on their feet, and to beat the drum, blow the bugle, strike up the band.

Eisenhower was startled and deeply hurt when he stepped down from his reviewing stand and was given a razzberry instead of a salute. But where he was rooted in the benevolent philosophy of the nineteenth century, a direct descendant in more ways than one of Herbert Hoover, Kennedy is the heir of the New Deal. Eisenhower personally did not even believe in the minimum-wage law. Yet he was not a reactionary. Those in his party who were put great pressure on him to turn back the clock. But he, faithful to remembered benevolence, insisted on letting it run on by itself in its own way.

The Secretary of Labor in Detroit.
In the background, Walter Reuther.

Kennedy is not reviewing the parade, but running around in it, not out of desire to get everybody in step but to help everybody hear the music. That is what the efforts on the domestic front of his first 100 days add up to.

THE MUSIC of the parade had been hitting clinkers periodically throughout the postwar period, but April 1960 was when it got off one that made the hair stand up on end.

On the fifth of that month, Kennedy won the primary in Wisconsin, then went on without pause to make his race in West Virginia, snapping his fingers between stops, crying, "Let's go, let's go." His campaign aides were sticking their heads out of the automobiles to shout the same thing at the traffic lights every time they turned red. "Come on, let's go. Let's go, here. Let's *go!*"

But in the Census Bureau, where the facts of national life are tabulated daily, the acres upon acres of high-speed computers with their insanely rapid winkings and stutterings were discussing other matters.

March had dumped down a whole winter of snow and bitter cold; it had made April an eagerly awaited event, and April was wonderfully warm, up to 92 degrees in Philadelphia, 86 in New York and Sacramento. Yet the sap had begun running out of the economy. People had stopped buying the goods from which are made the goods that make the goods people buy for their own consumption. Pleasure boats were selling fast, but not the ore and wood of which they were made.

Such twists in the American story have been normal, but the timing of this one was disconcertingly abnormal. From 1930 to 1945 had been the lean years of depres-

sion and war. Then had come a shopping spree so gorgeous it was unbelievable.

America became one great supermarket filled with astounding goodies. From Maine to the sun-kissed shores of Hawaii, the people came, spilling over with money, went off spilling over with bundles, to return again and again, endlessly, ceaselessly.

Meanwhile, the biggest worry of the factory managers, I learned in talking to them around the country, was the third shift. Those who worked from midnight to 8:00 A.M. just didn't maintain the same rate of production as the other two shifts. Perhaps they were tired. Perhaps it was the imps and gnomes that come to dance for a worker while his boss sleeps. Whatever it was, the factories that didn't have to stay open for their machines' sake grudgingly, reluctantly, rested eight hours a day. But that was all they rested.

We are not the materialistic people Europeans think. It's been true from the very beginning in this country: labor, expensive; materials, cheap—the direct opposite of anything known before, or yet known in many nations. Human hands, dear; the things they worked on, even the tools with which they worked, inexpensive. Now men are always paid on the basis of what they produce. It was true of cave men and remains true of Communists and capitalists. Yet in America, as production rose, work hours fell. We wanted it that way and had to fight our employers hard to get it.

It has been figured out that if Americans today were still working their grandfathers' hours, they would now be earning an *average* wage in excess of $25,000 a year, so greatly has productivity risen. (In 1889, the average production in one hour of one worker was, averaging it out in all non-farm industries, only 41.1 per cent of what it was in 1929. Today it's about 195 per cent of what it was in 1929.) But Americans prefer less money and more leisure—an average wage of $4,500 a year, an average work week below 40 hours.

Time, time — the only irreplaceable wealth. People want to spend it on their own. Yet this passion for less work stemmed neither the making nor the purchase of goods in the 1945–1960 period. Oh, it was a grand dance all right, with the very earth of the continent jigging away under the merry stamping of the factories.

For the first three years it seemed only natural. A long poverty had been ended by new riches. But it kept on and on. Men like myself, who had heard Herbert Hoover refer to the disastrous post-World War I shopping spree as "a new plateau," were made quite nervous.

Still, one had to admit, the New Deal had followed and, to support it, the income tax—had suddenly become the greatest force of all for distributing the wealth being produced. Had the new social organization of the country enabled the incredible new technology to lift our economy onto what actually was an unyielding new plateau?

It seemed possible. President Hoover had been a professional engineer. He understood the capacities of the new technology to push the economy onto such a plateau. Had his been an error merely in social philosophy, a failure to understand that the machines could not work in a vacuum, that the social system must be changed to match? So the New Dealers insisted. But had they been right? Was this "unnaturally" long prosperity the natural way of life on the new plateau, or was it just the same old balloon remaining airborne somewhat longer?

I remember asking George Humphrey the question. "I don't know," he replied, and him with his hands on the air valves of the balloon as Eisenhower's Secretary of the Treasury. "Who can be sure?" he concluded at great length. If not he, who indeed? Right after the war ended, Bernard Baruch had told me: "We are not going to have a depression for seven years." When 1952 passed, I heaved a sigh of relief. But, tiptoeing from Secretary Humphrey's office, I was more nervous than ever.

There were cycles, periods when the great engine of the economy slowed, but each time it spurted up again to work even better. The students tell me there has never been an economy without such cycles. They had them before the Middle Ages. They have them under the most rigid planning in Russia. But the cycles had become different—very different from the cataclysmic stallings and crashes we used to have, as a glance at the cycles of the last decade shows.

The first slow-down followed the Korean armistice, July 26, 1953, when so many factories had to reorganize for peacetime operations. By the fall of '54, the great engine was roaring more vigorously than it had during the high point of the Korean War.

I remember being in Cleveland that winter, feeling that America was even more insane than usual. On the one hand, the automobile workers were putting in overtime and Sundays to pile up enough money to go on strike. On the other hand, the plant managers were giving them as much overtime as they wanted—to pile up enough cars for the same strike. But the public kept grabbing the automobiles as fast as they were made. It ended the strike before it began.

It was not until 1957 that the engine started to slow down again. To economists, it was an "inventory recession." Economists define inventories as production beyond the level of final demand, meaning purchase. It is this kind of production that has made cycles an inevitable feature of any economy. For it takes time for the man at the raw-materials end of the assembly line to discover he's producing more than the customers at the other end are buying. Great attention is being paid now to how to use computers to shorten the time, and they have shortened it greatly. But the news still has to go from the public to the retailer to the wholesaler to the supplier to the assembler to the convertor to the manufacturer to the producer of the raw materials, and each of them has to have his own inventory so that orders may be filled promptly as they come in.

So again, in 1957, the economy had outpaced itself. No money had yet drained out of the public's pocket. It was just that the goods had been shoved into the pipeline faster than they could come out. But now the money began to drain. Workers at the far end of the line were laid off, or put on short week. Final demand for the so-called "big-ticket items"—consumer durables, paid for over a long period—slackened. Naturally enough, since the outlook for the future of more and more people was becoming uncertain.

Yet final demand for the consumer perishables (vacations, food, clothing, golf balls, all things paid for out of pocket or on short-term credit) continued high. This is the new feature of the post-1945 cycles. In the past, once the plug was pulled from any section of the area of final demand, it all began to drain. Today something the economists call "transfer payments" comes to the rescue. Transfer payments are defined as money that is paid over at a time when the work that earned it is not being done. They have always existed—for the few. But now, since the New Deal, they exist for the many who get social security, welfare, unemployment insurance, pensions, annuities. All those enriched by government social measures, taken under prodding from the people of our generation, and the lovely, golden fringe benefits granted largely under the prodding of the income tax and the moral influence that a high-wage economy exerts, kept emptying the pipeline undaunted.

But transfer payments go mostly to the old and unemployed, and this does not directly affect the final demand for the "big-ticket items." Working in their sector alone, the transfer payments come only indirectly and gradually to the rescue of the pipeline as a whole. At least, they always had before. Would they now? Were they actually enough in themselves to clear a pipeline clogged in the way this one was? Or would it be safer to man the government pumps and offer direct rescue to the parts of the economy affected?

In the first three months of 1958, a great debate began in Washington. Many of our leaders have never been able to bring themselves to believe in the reality of the new system. They've been living by it for thirty years now, but it's still a dream to them from which they are sure they will wake up some day to discover what they've known all along—that only gold is real, and credit not based on gold is just air.

To them it's all a balloon, supported only by the faith of the people in its soundness. Their faith is the only thing that has given gold its value, but, somehow, that's different. It's something they feel and therefore it's real —to them. Pumping anything further into the balloon, they are convinced, will make everybody lose faith in the balloon's soundness and rush to convert credit into real cash, precipitating a depression that, in George Humphrey's words, "will curl your hair."

At the end of the debate, the Administration, as was its wont, decided to do essentially nothing. Just as the opposition were winding up to roar, the economy took their breath away. Transfer payments had done the trick again. The pipeline was free and running.

The country settled down to another three years of bliss. But less than a year later, on July 15, 1959, the steel strike began.

This was the exact opposite of an inventory recession. The number of basic products with which modern industry does all its creating can be counted on the fingers, and steel, in its hundreds of varieties, is nearly one-third of them. Yet the manufacture of steel did not resume until November 7, one hundred and fifteen days later. The Administration had stuck to its hands-off policy that long. The strike had been the longest the industry had ever had. Even then it was not over, merely enjoying an 80-day Taft-Hartley breather. Under those circumstances, the baby boom remained in the incubator.

But with an election coming on, something had to be done about getting it out of there. Finally, on January 4, Vice-President Nixon managed to do it. Labor and management agreed on a contract.

"I acted under instructions from President Eisenhower," Nixon announced reverently and with sagacious modesty. "Without the Vice-President, we would not have had a settlement," proclaimed Secretary of Labor Mitchell, to make the voters realize that the heir to the General's place in the reviewing stand had feet of his own.

They were all so sure. Why not? The day the strike ended—click!—like clockwork the boom started. By March there were even those who were bored with it, and wondered: is that all there is to American life, an interminable whaling of the stuffings out of the same old dead dragons, want and scarcity? A mass-circulation magazine was so moved by the monotony of it all that it published a series of articles to remind America that somewhere around here, if only it could be found, there had once been a National Purpose. Where, oh where, was it now?

But in April, only three months after it had been pulled out of the incubator, the big, fat, juicy, boring boom began to disappear. "A rolling recession," said the

economists, "a sideways adjustment." But it kept walking out on us anyway.

Workers began dropping all over the country in thousands, then millions. We had a general. We were an army. But the general had never told us there was a war on. Who the hell was doing the shooting?

THE Constitution requires the President to be "a natural-born citizen" of the United States. It's a perceptive provision, a recognition of the profound place that place itself has in the forming of a man. We want a President who has been informed in his heart by the same national experiences that informed our hearts. Else he cannot sympathize, in any sophisticated sense, with our values, or even know what they are.

Here's an example: I had lunch last March in Houston with a group of wealthy oil men. Say "creeping socialism" and they roar automatically, but so strenuously it comes out as a squeak. Yet they roar with just as great pain at the idea that they pay tolls to keep the barge canal the Government has built along the Gulf Coast from being what it is, a socialistic act. Who but someone who has had America as his school could understand what the word "socialism" has come to mean in this country, and sympathize with the oil men's 360-degree pain?

During the Washington hearings on the new minimum-wage law, I listened to the opposition from the Chamber of Commerce, the National Association of Manufacturers and other associations of businessmen. Here were the gallant old soldiers who never die, simply fade away. They used the same words—ruinous, unconstitutional, states' rights, inflation, free enterprise—that they have been using for nearly thirty years now, in opposing a minimum wage that was at first a mere twenty-five cents an hour, then fifty, seventy-five, ninety and, at the moment they had flung themselves into battle again, one dollar. Who but one who had grown up among these men could understand the concrete things their abstract words meant to them? Every American knows very definitely what he means, even in this day, by "free enterprise." He knows even what another American means, by the context in which he uses the phrase and the tone in which he pronounces it. It's not something that can be learned by studying abroad.

The Constitution also requires a President to have been "fourteen years a resident within the United States." But, alas, it does not stipulate which century.

The early years are the vital ones. Then it is that a man gets his conceptions of what the world is like and how he himself, to discover his own identity, can change it, put a mark on it rather than just let it mark him. The time when those years were lived was not a matter of political significance when the Constitution was composed. In fact, in all the centuries until the twentieth, any man could reasonably expect to die in a world that had changed in very few important ways since he was born. The conceptions he had formed in youth were adequate to cope with the situations confronting him in old age. But in this century the whole world changes on a man between one pair of glasses and another.

The economy I studied as a youth is not at all the economy I must understand today. A saying I've been hearing is that the American society has undergone more fundamental changes in the last thirty years than in the three hundred since the white man first began tearing down the forest. If that's true, I told myself, then I ought to be able to know that it is without looking out the window, without moving from this desk.

I looked at what I was holding in my hand—a pen. What social changes have come about in the last thirty years to affect so common a writing instrument more than it has been affected in the last three hundred?

To begin with, my handwriting is poor because I'm indifferent to it. I grew up using a typewriter. Then there's the market for writing instruments. The American experiment of mass compulsory education took hold more slowly than is generally realized. By 1870, only 2 per cent of the population seventeen years old were high-school graduates; by 1900 a mere 6 per cent. In the three hundred American years until 1930, it got up to 29 per cent. Then it took off and soared, rising thirty-four points in the next thirty years. Today, 63 per cent of the seventeen-year-olds of all our races and colors are high-school graduates, and 40 per cent of our people are or have been in college.

It doesn't really have to be carried any further. But my pen happens to be a ball-point. When I think of how it was put together from parts made all over the United States with machines, techniques and discoveries about the nature and properties of materials from the whole civilization, I have to concede the statement is correct. America's long day of independence has ended. It is July 5 now for all of us, the day of interdependence.

The story of the "soft spots" in the economy is typical. How did they happen? Well, in 1955, 65 per cent of the Corning Glass Company's business, its president, George Decker, told me, was done by selling products that had not been in existence in 1945. This has been the rule in all industries, not the exception. Naturally, those whose economic destinies were committed to the old products suffered.

But more than mere commodities became out-of-date. Railroads—almost a nation of industries in themselves—lost their roles as universal carriers. A terrible whittling began, a slashing and grinding down to fit into a smaller, more specialized groove. So, the country's scores and hundreds of railroad towns—the depots and junctions, the repair and supply centers—that had sprung up and flourished for a hundred years became "soft spots," too.

In a more sophisticated, wealthier nation, automobiles lost their appeal as status symbols. More size, more horsepower, the grossness of the Cadillac dream began going the way of the overstuffed sofa and with it that "planned obsolescence" of tail fins upon which the factories and dealers relied for a large proportion of their sales of new cars.

When Henry Wallace was Secretary of Agriculture, one American farmer fed eleven people and created a surplus. Today, with the population less than half again as large as it was then, one farmer is feeding more than twice as many—twenty-five. Today it takes only 200,000 miners to produce the same amount of coal as 600,000 of their fathers produced, and John L. Lewis sees the trend accelerating. In his opinion, a mere 50,000 miners is all the country really needs.

Thus the "soft spots." Down in West Virginia in April 1960, Kennedy stuck his finger in one "soft spot" and held up the ooze for everybody to see. It was rotten.

In the richest nation in the world at a time of its greatest prosperity and *interdependence,* children were bringing their school lunches home to feed their parents. That was just plain rottenness, the same kind that put Coxey's Army on the march in 1894 (to be arrested in Washington for "trespassing on the grass") and brought the country to the edge of anarchy under Herbert Hoover.

But on Pennsylvania Avenue (suddenly, under Eisenhower, become an extension of Madison Avenue) they kept using the nice, soft, cushiony phrase for it: "soft spot." It lulled the people into feeling comfortable about it all.

The fact is, the Republican Administration didn't see any use to be gained from waking people. In their view of "free enterprise" a business's business was the business only of those directly involved. True, many of them had progressed to the point where they included the employees among those directly involved. But let them manage their own show in their own way and keep the people out of it.

Basically, they had no faith in the people. There was a kind of rough justice in what happened to them in the Presidential election as a result. For it was their lack of faith in people that gave Kennedy his great tactical advantage of the campaign—the religious issue. Kennedy landed on it in the same masterly fashion as Eisenhower on Normandy, and his opposition deserved it.

Mistrust of Catholics vanished as a national political issue long ago, when industry came out of the jungle. It survived only as a memory among minority groups, a fear of a ghost that might yet walk again. Even in 1928 the issue was politically dead. A wonderful man, Alfred E. Smith, was rejected as President not because he was a Catholic but because he was a Democrat (in a Republican country at the time of the heyday of the party), a wet (in a dry nation) and, unabashedly, a New Yorker who said "woiker" and "terl" (in a country that suspected all its cities, and New York most of all). It's a tribute to this extraordinary personality that Smith came as close as he did—fifteen million votes to Hoover's twenty-one million.

The bishops who lined up against Kennedy, as analysis of the returns showed, did not speak for their flock. Nixon had only to look in his own heart to realize it. But it takes faith in people to read them by looking into your own heart.

It was obvious that unless Nixon prevented the Catholic vote from rallying behind Kennedy as a bloc, he would lose the Northeast and the election. He had only to devote a major speech to the issue, exposing it for the nonsense it had become. But he had no faith, not in Protestants or Catholics—no faith in people, in their reaction to truth.

Instead, he had faith in the slick savvy of Madison Avenue. Rather than fight the issue, he told it to go away. The immediate reaction among Catholics was: See, the issue exists. If he won't fight it, we must, by

voting for Kennedy. When that reaction stimulated Nixon to remain silent, they said: See, he's willing to let "them" help him. Poor fellow, he felt caught between a cough and a sneeze.

In the meantime, Kennedy, a very able, rough political infighter, never let go, and in the end the unreal issue actually did lick Nixon. Some 62 per cent of the Catholic Republicans, the largest single bloc to desert the Eisenhower camp, voted for Kennedy. Analysis shows that the Republicans did not lose in the cities (where they had never won in '52 and '56) but in the suburbs where the more prosperous Catholics lived.

It is not often that we see a man of little faith routed from the palace of half-truth, but we did in 1960.

Fundamentally, the Eisenhower Administration was composed of decent-minded, intelligent, well-informed, devotedly responsible nineteenth-century paternalists. They had the nation's best interests at heart. They set an unusually high moral tone. But every time circumstances forced them to deal with America as an interdependent society, they had to go into action with their conception of what such a society is. The mothballs and old dust flew.

An illustration is the steel strike. Here was no dispute over nickels and dimes. Great Steel, Mighty Steel was in danger of becoming another "soft spot." A year before the nation itself had heard the phrase, it had come to the new frontier. Ahead lay uncharted country, acreep with the unknown, the unpredictable. How best might a multitude progress there? The Captains of Management had their ideas, the Captains of Labor different ones and, since they lacked any national direction, they drew the sword.

The Administration, clinging to the nineteenth century, waited interminably — one hundred and fifteen days! Then all it did was to get a court to order the quarreling factions to stand in a corner and see if that cooled off their temper tantrum.

Did they think that that would beat the sword, unsheathed in so urgent a cause, into a plowshare? It only hung it up over the rest of the economy as a Sword of Damocles. Then, even when they forced a truce under the pressure of events, they still provided no national direction, merely got the disputants to ignore the central issue and to try resuming business as usual.

So steel became a "soft spot." In what the calendar said should have been the fifteenth fat year, following the fifteen lean, business as usual went on only for three months. The workers who had been told to go back to work were told to go home.

But now the voice of Kennedy is heard in the land, and his snapping fingers, his cry of "Let's go, let's go."

L ET'S GO where?

"I like your President," said Prime Minister Macmillan after he had met him. "He catches on to ideas very fast."

I watched Secretary of Agriculture Freeman carry on a heated dispute over the intercom on his desk while reading and signing his mail and wig-wagging instructions on other matters to his secretary. (The man on the other end of the intercom was one of those slow-hemming drawlers and he left long micro-seconds between words.) Secretary of Labor Goldberg could hardly find time to attend his own swearing-in and merely popped his head in at the punch-bowl party he gave for four hundred of his staff.

"You know, they call me the old man of the Cabinet," I was told by Secretary of Commerce Luther Hodges, a vigorous 63, probably the most impressive, certainly the most charming and cultivated man in it. "That means I just have to make more things happen faster than anybody."

The words from Kennedy to his aides have been: "Don't knock down any fence until you find out why it was put up." Yet in his first three months he has flooded Congress with bills (16) and messages (16), and has broken the power of the conservative House Rules Committee to prevent consideration of bills they don't like.

Few of the bills offer anything new. In fact, three of the more important—extension of unemployment benefits, the rise in minimum wages, and aid to depressed areas—were tried for in the Eisenhower Administration by Secretary of Labor Mitchell.

But Mitchell tried to do it without the people. Now Secretary of Labor Goldberg had dragged the whole country into it, carried the press with him, dramatized, shouted *Fire!*

And even now the Eisenhower team is convinced it is an inadvisable thing to do. "It weakens confidence" is the gist of their argument. "It makes the situation look worse than it is."

So it has, to those who have remained both prosperous and uninformed. But if you have faith in people, you have faith in businessmen, too, faith at least in their capacity to remain informed about their own business. Goldberg's faith is not misplaced. While he has been running around "destroying their confidence" with all his might, the stock market has begun to rise and keeps rising, orders for inventory have begun to climb, factories have started extending the work week. When you are in a building and smell smoke, hear crackling sounds, see flames, which gives you more confidence: reassuring words that it's only mice, or the clang of fire engines?

In a story, now classic, it is told how the manager of the Ford plant took Walter Reuther of the UAW through to show him a new machine, 1500 feet long, that performed 530 separate, intricate operations to transform a piece of iron into a finished engine block. "Well, Walter," the manager said, "how are you going to make that machine join your union?" "How are you going to make it buy a Ford car?" replied Reuther.

In an interdependent society, there *must* be full employment. The classes break down. It is happening in Western Europe. (In England, they are now referring to their "upper classless.") It has already happened here. The good of one *must* be the concern of all. Prosperity is indivisible.

It takes getting used to. But to see what's been happening in our society, we have only to realize, in all its beauty and difficulty, what's happened to our farms. Food, clothing, shelter—these are the foundations of any society, and all the food and most of the clothing come from the farm.

In 1900, 60 per cent of our population was rural, living in unincorporated places. They put 319 million acres to crops, 276 million acres in pasture. The population of the U.S. was 76 million. Today, with 180 million people, we're using very little more cropland (399 million acres) but twice as much pasture (526 million acres). It seems we've changed over from the beans-and-bread diet of 1900. But the point is that 3 million farms in the United States are grossing over $5,000 a year. The bulk of our food and fibers is produced on about 800,000 farms. The rest are worked by moonlighters, adding to

their town-earned income, or puttering greens for hobbyists.

A similar fate looms now for the mass-production industries. It happened first on farms for obvious reasons. Nature needs only understanding to step up her production; earth-moving and materials-handling (the basic work of farmers) can be speeded up dazzlingly by relatively uncomplicated applications of mechanical power. But the days of the mass-producers as mass-employers are numbered too. One has only to see the new machines in actual use now, or on the near horizon, to realize that there's almost no end to what machines can do better than semi-skilled or even skilled human hands, no end to what computers can make them do better than human managers.

It's a second industrial revolution, as wide and deep as the first. It confronts our generation with a novel problem: how to keep busy. We are confronted with an embarrassment of riches.

It's no mere discomposure, as King Midas learned, and he was concerned only with himself. We're a nation of 180 million free-enterprisers with sacred and inalienable rights as individuals. But free enterprise is the goose that laid the golden egg and the problem is dividing the egg, not the goose.

In the spring of 1961, the Kennedy Administration offered a new pair of gloves to King Midas on the farm. Will it solve the situation? Probably not. Will it ease it? It ought to, when Congress finally finishes with it. After all, we have now had considerable experience from which to learn.

But there is no solution, actually. For neither in part nor over-all is it a problem. It is life itself, a new kind of life, streaming pell-mell from what was to what will be.

Some intimations of the new life are already visible. Every year now more than twelve million people move their homes at least as far as to another county. We migrate from industry to industry, too. In most groups of men engaged in almost any kind of work, those who started out in life expecting to do that work and training themselves for it are now the exception rather than the rule.

Everybody used to regard himself as a native of a particular state. Now that's becoming irrelevant for more and more of us. Moving from state to state, two years here and one year there, we are natives of the whole continent. America is our home.

The man who starts out in tugboats can work the heavy machinery on land too, and does. Thousands of graduate engineers are now in sales or management. I've met more corporation executives who were hired away from other corporations in other fields than rose in their own fields. Here is George Bunker, head of the billion-dollar Martin Company. He went from the Massachusetts Institute of Technology into the grocery business, then to truck trailers and airplanes, and now he's in the space business. That kind of hopping around is normal procedure nowadays. We are all becoming interchangeable parts in the interdependent American enterprise.

It's a process that has left a lot of unfinished business in its wake and finds a great deal more business barely begun. The White House can only confront the people with their national tasks. But in his first 100 days the President has started in that direction. He said, Let's go—and, brother, it looks as though we ought to buy a ticket.

Jess Mullenniex, cut back to a three-day work week, tells Goldberg that he faces bankruptcy.

Mullenniex, with nineteen years' seniority in a woolen mill, cannot tell his story to Goldberg without emotion.

Behind the files of unemployment compensation claims, some of the men whose names are on file.

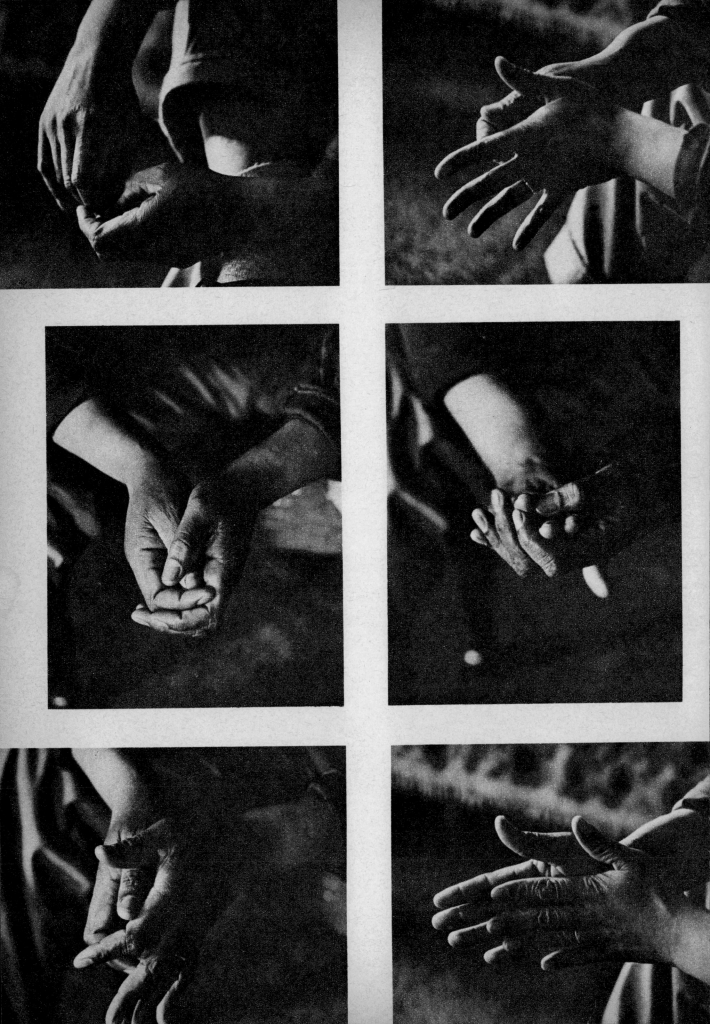

Unemployment compensation office

depressed area

Photographed by ELLIOTT ERWITT

Unsold cars

Waiting for food distribution at a welfare center in Detroit.

Food distribution of Federal surplus products in the North Woodward section. No sugar: this is a luxury.

The line-up for unemployment checks.

OPPOSITE

An unemployed miner walks the tracks past a row of empty and idle railroad cars and an inoperative tipple once used to sort and wash the coal.

WEST VIRGINIA

Photographed by CONSTANTINE MANOS

Unemployed miners receive
monthly government surplus food

"All this will not be finished in the first 100 days. Nor will it be finished in the first 1,000 days, nor in the life of this Administration, nor even perhaps in our lifetime on this planet.

BUT LET US BEGIN

By SIDNEY HYMAN and MARTIN AGRONSKY

Photographed by DENNIS STOCK

THERE WERE many beginnings. Which was the first?

In the beginning was the word—voiced by John F. Kennedy at a National Press Club luncheon in January 1960, soon after he became a declared candidate for the Democratic Presidential nomination. Before he rose to speak, the reporters in their table-talk wondered how the man could ever win the party nomination, let alone the White House. He was very young, a Catholic of Irish descent, a United States Senator, a big-city product—five "thou shall nots" American political parties traditionally bore in mind when picking their Presidential candidates. It was therefore expected that at the Press Club luncheon Senator Kennedy would hurl an artificial rainbow across the sky—as if the illusion would lift the clouds from his prospects.

Senator Kennedy did the unexpected.

He spoke not about himself but about the Presidency— how it had come of late to creak like a body whose life is leaving, and how it had to be revived if the nation was to be led safely through the stormy 1960s which lay ahead.

First of all, said he, there had to be a return to the Constitutional concept which makes the President "the vital center of action in the American scheme of government." This in turn meant many things. It meant a President who was "a vigorous proponent of the national interest, not a passive broker for conflicting private interests." It meant a man "capable of acting as the commander-in-chief of the Grand Alliance, not merely a bookkeeper who feels that his work is done when the numbers on the balance sheet come out even." It meant a President who would be "the head of a responsible party, not rise so far above politics as to be invisible; a man who would formulate and fight for legislative policies, not a casual bystander to the legislative process."

Six months after this was said, Senator Kennedy won the Democratic Presidential nomination on the first ballot. Ten months after the same thing was resaid by him wherever men stopped to listen, Senator Kennedy became President-elect Kennedy at midday of November 7, 1960.

Here was another beginning.

Victory, though won by only half the votes, led in a direct train to all the prizes, to all the problems—and to a question about responsible power. Would Mr. Kennedy's acts now stand as one with his words about how a President must act? Or would a recurrent divorce in the Eisenhower Presidency afflict his own as well? Would the ringing manifestos of good intentions issued from the rear of the battle line seem unrelated to what was done or left undone at the front of real events? The full answer would have to hang in suspense until Mr. Kennedy took the Presidential oath of office. But within the four corners of what he was free to do as a President-elect, he served early notice that, as President, he would strive to make his acts be like limbs extending from his words.

The notice unfolded in a point-counterpoint response to challenges.

He saw the immediate need to clear the air of election-time rancors. So there followed the symbolic act of a gallant call on his defeated rival, Mr. Richard Nixon.

He saw the immediate need to assure the nation that there would be no jolts when the levers of power changed hands on Inauguration Day. So he arranged for "Kennedy men" to work with their opposite numbers in the Eisenhower Presidency on plans for an orderly shift between Administrations.

AFFAIRS in the Eisenhower years taught Kennedy not to think that a spontaneous combustion of happy air would lead to agreements with the Russians—or that the agreements would be made to stick through the adhesive of cosmic bubble gum publicly chewed at summit meetings. Indeed, after the 1960 collapse of "summitry," it was not clear where—if anywhere—there was room for serious conversations with the Russians about Cold War issues. Yet, as a new beginning had to be made, one at least could try to create and maintain a climate where it might be possible to discover if there were any specific points the Russians were prepared to bring into the area of serious negotiations.

A first chance to help create such a climate came within hours after Mr. Kennedy was named the victor in the 1960 Presidential contest, and there was delivered to his Hyannisport headquarters a cable of congratulations from the Soviet Premier, Mr. Khrushchev. State Department experts who were consulted about the reply advised a one-sentence answer and warned against a trap if more was said.

Mr. Kennedy respected the force of the warning but not the advice preceding it.

He reasoned that a single-sentence reply would seem brusque at the receiving end and that a fuller, more courteous reply could be framed without in any way weakening one's position. Brusqueness itself would add nothing to America's own strength and security. It would not keep the Russians confined to the United Nations—and out of Africa or anywhere else. It would raise Mr. Khrushchev's hackles at first contact with him. It would freeze the air. It would persuade the onlooking neutrals that it was the fixed purpose of the incoming Administration to raise hell just for the hell of it.

The precisely framed reply the President-elect eventually sent to the Soviet leader on November 7 was friendly but not innocent in tone. It expressed the hope that the two men could concert their efforts in a new search for peace, but in no way did it accept at face value any Russian vows of good intentions.

A small matter, yes. Yet in capsule form it contained most of the elements of style that were to mark Mr. Kennedy's approach to East-West issues during his first 100 days as President. There would be no public posture of verbal belligerency, no default on substantive points, and no childlike belief that in international matters

"good will" is somehow self-executing. There would be a steady address to the complex task of making oneself less menacing to the Soviet Union and at the same time stronger in dealing with them. There would be a new respect for the opinions of neutral powers—and a veering away from the seesaw concept that a neutral who received marks of friendship from the Soviet Union thereby became a self-confessed enemy of the United States.

The day after the reply was dispatched to Mr. Khrushchev, President-elect Kennedy turned his full attention to another matter. He wanted no loss of momentum and no leadership vacuum of the kind that was suffered when President Eisenhower entered the White House in 1953 with little more than a plan to appoint "study groups." But in his own case, where was the compass by which he could navigate the greasy sea of troubles awaiting him the instant he took his Presidential oath? Mr. Kennedy's long service in the Congress had, of course, acquainted him with the history of many problems he would soon have to face in the White House. Moreover, as a candidate for the Democratic Presidential nomination, and then as a Presidential nominee, he had consumed acres of facts bearing on every question before the nation. All this was helpful, but it was not an action program set down in detail. Known things still had to be amplified, given specific form and an order of priority in which they would be fought for.

THUS on Thursday, November 8, the President-elect held a day-long meeting with a group of young men who had been his closest campaign aides and who are identified here by their present positions: Attorney General Robert Kennedy, Special Counsel Theodore Sorensen, Appointment Secretary Kenneth O'Donnell, Press Secretary Pierre Salinger and Special Assistant for Congressional Relations Lawrence O'Brien. It was at this meeting that the President-elect made Sorensen responsible for putting together the machinery that could help formulate an action program. This in turn led to a further decision that special task forces would be formed, each to deal with a special subject on a list compiled by the President-elect and Sorensen.

Sorensen soon staffed fifteen such task forces and had them at work under a clear-cut set of instructions. They were to isolate the issues in their field of inquiry; propose lines of action necessary and suitable for Mr. Kennedy to take as President; suggest where a proposed course of action could swing on an Executive Order alone and where it required Congressional action.

With this under way, Mr. Kennedy turned his attention to yet another matter. He had thoroughly studied the defects of the Eisenhower Presidency as an executive and was clear in his own mind about what to avoid and what to seek in his own Presidential apparatus. He would avoid entrapping his power of decision in a rigid staff system, in a maze of interagency committees, or in a formalized Cabinet. He would find and recruit for his Administration men who could bring high professional competence and an authentic political mentality to their posts but who would also fit in with Mr. Kennedy's ideas about how he personally meant to work as President.

He meant to be, in fact as well as in theory, the Secretary in Charge of all the Secretaries. In all great and essential matters, therefore, he would make the organic decisions—and hold himself personally accountable for the over-all results.

What he wanted from his appointees, wherever placed, was a special kind of help—to spot problems before they came in crisis form, to frame alternative solutions to those problems, to bring to the moment of decision the strongest case for and against any proposed course of action. In formulating policy he would work with small task forces of men most immediately involved in a particular matter. But once a Presidential policy was decided on, specific individuals would be held personally responsible for the faithful execution and supervision of that policy.

Mr. Kennedy kept his own counsel about the particular individuals he meant to bring into his Administration, if available. But to help enlarge his vision, lists of the main jobs to be filled and the special skills required of those who would fill them were compiled by Clark Clifford and Richard Neustadt, the President-elect's representatives in dealing with the Eisenhower Administration on the problems of transition. Also, he had his brother-in-law, Sargent Shriver, now the head of the Peace Corps, direct a team of talent scouts—Ralph Dungan and Harris Wofford, now Special Assistants in the White House, and Adam Yarmolinsky, now an Assistant Secretary of Defense—who sought out, processed and brought to Mr. Kennedy's notice many scores of individuals worthy of consideration as appointees to the new Administration.

In their collective character, the appointments actually made by Mr. Kennedy were fundamentally different from those made by General Eisenhower when he entered the White House. In the latter case, a striking number of General Eisenhower's Cabinet and sub-Cabinet members had been on the Business Advisory Council of the Department of Commerce, or had direct business and professional connections with the leading corporation executives comprising that council. In Mr. Kennedy's case, by contrast, the appointees came from everywhere—from universities, Governors' mansions, the Congress, from business, labor and farm circles, from the philanthropic foundations—and thus were a transcript of American life as a whole.

WHILE THE prospective members of Mr. Kennedy's Administration were being found and fitted into place, the task forces appointed earlier to work on designated policy questions were completing their work. As these reached Sorensen's hands, he isolated the issues they raised and spotted places where a proposal could lead to further conflicts and problems. A compendium of policy decisions to be made was then prepared by him and became the subject of a day-long meeting held early in late December between the President-elect, Sorensen and four other men. Identified by their present posts, they were Deputy Special Counsel Myer Feldman, a long-time aide; Budget Director David Bell; Deputy Budget Director Elmer Staats; and Presidential Adviser Richard Neustadt.

Mr. Kennedy emerged from this meeting with a set of decisions about which matters he would take up first as President and which would be postponed for the time being. But central to all these was the decision he made about the approach he would take to the economy. Along with other liberal Democrats in the immediately preceding years, he accepted the need for Federal leadership in the development of natural resources, housing, urban renewal, medical care for the aged, aid to education, defense and foreign aid. In his election campaign he had expressly called for a higher and more sustained rate of economic growth that could pay for such a Federal investment. At the same time he knew that while over-all production was $500 billion annually, the U.S. had an existing capacity to produce $550 billion annually—and that the $50 billion gap between where we *were* and where we *had to be* first had to be closed before there could be any natural inducement for further growth.

At this point there entered a complication that is best seen through the force of a historical comparison. Where the total collapse of the economy in 1933 spoke its own permission for "bold experimentation," the 1961 slip was not so widely felt as to evoke a nation-wide outcry for heroic remedies. Even minimal remedies would be fought in quarters held captive in their thinking by the ongoing power of the Eisenhower Administration's budget-balancing simplicities. Mr. Kennedy, therefore, drew certain conclusions as he estimated the political side of the economic case. To consolidate the public's trust in his own "fiscal responsibility," his initial budgetary requests would be modest. They would be addressed in the main to taking up the slack in the unemployment. If they succeeded in doing this by the fall of 1961, then would be the time for a more fundamental attack on the many other things that were amiss in the economic system.

The economic decision just sketched in—along with the other decisions reached by Mr. Kennedy in late December—was communicated to each Cabinet officer by the team of Sorensen, Feldman, Bell and Staats. They asked each Cabinet member to review the Eisenhower budget as it affected his department, and to bear several considerations in mind when doing this. The Cabinet member was to defer all minor changes in the budget until a later date; recommend new policies (as in the case of foreign aid) that could be instituted without a resort to new appropriations; recommend new appropriations only when they were indispensable to a fundamental shift in policy (as was to prove the case in the fields of education and defense); and recommend how authorized funds could be disbursed more rapidly to stimulate an early economic recovery.

BY THESE many beginnings Mr. Kennedy reached the ultimate beginning of his oath-taking moment. He had already seized the initiative in giving form and focus to his Administration. He had already drawn around him a body of gifted men with a coherent view of where he wanted to go. He had already assured the nation that, despite his youth, he could be the undisputed captain on the bridge of the American leviathan. So now he saluted his oath-taking moment in an Inaugural Address that forged a common destiny between the voting constituency of his fellow Americans and his non-voting constituency around the world.

There is an arithmetical measure of how well Mr. Kennedy was prepared to begin to act out many of the decisions he had reached in the weeks between his election and the Inauguration. In the sixty days following his Inauguration, he issued thirty-two official messages and legislative recommendations, compared to five for Dwight D. Eisenhower in the same period and twenty-three for Franklin D. Roosevelt. He issued twenty-two proclamations and Executive Orders, compared to thirteen for Eisenhower and sixty-three for the crisis-ridden Roosevelt. He held seven press conferences, while Eisenhower had held four; Roosevelt, with a minute press corps to deal with, met the press twice a week, with the reporters banked around his desk. Kennedy also was deluged with 274,960 pieces of mail, while Eisenhower had received 195,000 pieces, half of which dealt with the Rosenberg case. Finally, Mr. Kennedy, in common with Roosevelt, missed no work days in Washington, while Eisenhower had missed four.

In all of this, besides the help he received from men like Special Counsel Sorensen, he was braced in incalculably important ways by three other strategically placed personal aides. One was Appointment Secretary Kenneth O'Donnell, who, besides regulating the flow of people, papers and problems to and from the President's desk, served as a one-man brigade dealing with spot emergencies. Another was Special Assistant for Congressional Relations Lawrence O'Brien, whose daily life was a ceaseless struggle to make the President's purposes prevail in the Congress. The third was Special Assistant for National Security Affairs McGeorge Bundy, whose daily task was to help the President master the explosive forces abroad all around the world.

As for Mr. Kennedy himself: the nation could not have known that he began in fact to be President of the United States even as the Inauguration Day parade was on. When the Coast Guard cadets marched past, he alone seemed to notice that there were no Negro cadets in the contingent. He made a mental note to ask why, and when the question was put to "the right people" they answered that there was only one Negro officer in the whole of the Coast Guard. When he again asked why, the answer had something to do with the entrance requirements at the Coast Guard Academy. Not many days after, in keeping with his "executive approach" to civil-rights matters, there followed quietly a Presidential remedy of direct benefit to all young Negroes who aspire to be officers in the Coast Guard.

If this new beginning went unnoticed, the case was different in another matter. At 9:00 A.M. of January 21, 1961—the first day of official work—the White House staff members were in the Fish Room awaiting their office-space assignment. The President himself sat in a bare office. But he called in Myer Feldman, his Deputy Special Counsel, and asked him to draft the text of an Executive Order that would carry out a campaign promise to increase the quantity and quality of the food distributed to the people in need. Feldman, who had been ready for this moment since the West Virginia primary, went off by himself and was back at 10:00 A.M. with a draft—which President Kennedy signed at 10:30 A.M. and issued at 11:00 A.M. as Executive Order No. 1.

Where other corners of the economic situation lent themselves to the stimulus of Executive action, the action was forthcoming. Thus, by Executive Order, there was a speed-up in the payment of tax refunds; in the disbursement of dividends on G.I. insurance; in the disbursement to the states of the entire balance of the Federal funds to help highway construction in the fiscal year; and a stepped-up pace of Federal construction on other projects for which funds were authorized. Also by Executive action there was a lowering of interest rates on Federally insured mortgage money for home construction; on loans for the construction of community facilities; and a start of a policy that looked to the lowering of long-term interest rates in the economy as a whole. The Secretary of Defense, meanwhile, was directed to channel defense contracts to areas with surplus labor. The Secretary of Agriculture was directed promptly to release to the Farm Home Administration authorized funds for farm home loans; to accelerate on an optional basis one half of the current payments due to the farmer for storage crops under price-support loans; and to establish pilot food-stamp programs in designated areas.

In a counterattack on the outward flow of gold that had panicked the Eisenhower Presidency in its last days, Mr. Kennedy "stabilized the atmosphere" by making plain to the world the massive resources the United States could throw into the breach in the event of need. He rescinded President Eisenhower's order which tried to stop the gold outflow by separating U.S. servicemen overseas from their families, and instead initiated measures to curtail the personal expenditures of overseas servicemen and their overseas dependents. To induce foreign governments and monetary authorities to hold their foreign official balances in dollars, the Secretary of the Treasury was empowered to use his existing authority to issue U.S. securities to these foreign official bodies at special rates of interest. And again steps were taken to create within the Department of Commerce a section that would encourage foreign tourism through publicizing in foreign capitals the advantages of a visit to America.

Beyond what could be done to halt the outward flow of gold by Executive Orders, supporting legislative measures were drafted for Congressional enactment. The Senate was prodded to approve U. S. membership in the Organization for Economic Cooperation and Development. The Congress was urged to provide funds for an expansion of U. S. overseas commercial facilities, to end the abuse of "tax havens" abroad by American investors, and to reduce customs exemptions for returning American travelers. On top of all this, Mr. Kennedy—as in the case of the West German Federal Republic—pressed the economically well-off countries of the free world to provide a fair share of economic help for underdeveloped nations.

While the gold outflow was being checked by these immediate or prospective steps, Mr. Kennedy used the mixed device of Executive Orders and legislative requests to deal with other aspects of the economic picture. Take the case of the Business Advisory Council of the Department of Commerce. Created in the time of Franklin D. Roosevelt, it had become a self-appointing, self-perpetuating group of men representing giant corporations who received privileged information in secret which they could then turn to their own advantage. This was changed by President Kennedy and his Secretary of Commerce, Luther Hodges. The members henceforth would be appointed by the Secretary of Commerce; they would include representatives of small business; and the meetings would be thrown open to the press.

MEANWHILE, to help maintain industrial peace on a basis fair to management, labor and the general public, President Kennedy, at the instigation of Secretary of Labor Arthur Goldberg, created a new Advisory Committee on Labor-Management policy. The Labor Department itself, once the stepchild among all government agencies, began to throb with new life. In a clean break with the practices of the Eisenhower Administration, it did not, for example, sit idly by while strikes developed and ran their crippling course. It became a direct and immediate participant in resolving labor-management problems as they arose, settling three major strikes successfully within a few weeks after Inauguration Day.

In other directions, it kept a close watch on the labor bill sponsored by Mr. Kennedy as a Senator, to see how it served the ends for which it was framed, and how it should be changed, if necessary. New personnel were added to the Department of Labor to bring expert knowledge to bear on the need to make employment security more diversified in the face of automation—and in the face of the long-term neglect suffered by older people who had lost their jobs but who could be relocated in places where their skills were needed, or who could be retrained under existing government programs.

The rehabilitation of the Labor Department by these and other means was paralleled by the work of Secretary Abraham Ribicoff in rehabilitating his Department of Health, Education and Welfare. The Office of Education was sharply upgraded in importance; steps were taken to modernize the Children's Bureau, and the whole gamut of social-security programs was re-examined to see whether they were abreast of the needs of the time.

Cutting across all this was President Kennedy's move by Executive action to end discrimination in employment opportunities. As a member of Congress he saw how often legislative efforts to improve the position of racial minorities were talked to death in the Senate. As President, therefore, he resolved to bypass the civil-rights burial and battleground in the Congress and to affirm, in Franklin D. Roosevelt's phrase, "the creative possibilities of the law." He had in mind the fact that existing laws applicable to the field of civil rights already contained an immense power for action. Used to the full by the Executive, their impact would dwarf the effects even of the strongest civil-rights bill the Congress might be induced to approve.

His intention to use those powers to the full was plainly indicated in an Executive Order of March 7, which established the President's Committee on Equal Employment Opportunity under the chairmanship of Vice President Lyndon Johnson, and with Secretary of Labor Goldberg as the more direct supervisor of the work done by that committee. The terms of the Executive Order called for non-discrimination in all government employment and covered all government contractors, sub-contractors and all labor unions whose members work on such contracts—meaning nearly a quarter of the American working force of some seventy million men and women. To this end, the Executive Order called for a report by early May which would provide for the first time a statistical breakdown by color of all those whose work entails the use of Federal funds; and second, the report was also to contain specific recommendations about how to deal with and remove the inequities revealed by the statistics on current employment patterns.

In the meantime, Attorney General Robert Kennedy began to show what Executive action in the area of civil rights could mean. He inherited the school desegregation mess in New Orleans, where the Eisenhower Administration not only refused a direct request for help but tried to persuade the sitting Federal judge to delay his own action until after the Presidential elections. Conduct of this kind emboldened the Louisiana House of Representatives to try by legislative means to block the Federal court's order for the payment of New Orleans' schoolteachers—but not after Attorney General Kennedy was sworn in and quietly went to work on the problem he inherited. The New Orleans schoolteachers were paid when he made it clear, first, that the Justice Department would stand behind the school board all the way; and second, that if the Louisiana House of Representatives continued to defy the court order, all the members might end in jail.

Without fanfare after that, the Justice Department made itself *amicus parti* to suits in four public-school desegregation cases introduced before the Federal court in Louisiana, thus serving notice at the outset that the petitioners had behind them the full power of the Federal government. Nor was this all. The Attorney General also let it be known that the Negro's right to vote would be unequivocally supported by the Department of Justice wherever violations of that right were brought into view —as could be the case in sixteen Southern counties where Negroes have population majorities but not one member of the race is registered to vote. The assumption throughout is that once the intention of the White House to provide civil-rights leadership is clearly shown, the ensuing new climate of opinion will, in itself, work positive results in the area of civil rights.

Aside from civil-rights matters, the Attorney General made some beginnings of his own in other areas of law enforcement. Convinced that the difficulty of dealing with organized crime is as much a matter of attitude as of law, he created a new section in the Justice Department to direct a co-ordinated Federal attack on national crime syndicates. He also presented to Congress a new plan designed to prevent juvenile delinquency, or to assist youthful offenders already in jail toward re-entry into society in ways that would not make them "criminal repeaters." Finally, to deal with respectable law-breakers, preparatory steps were taken to mount a major attack on price-fixing, with twenty-five newly recruited lawyers being added to the Justice Department's Antitrust Division for this purpose.

ALL THAT WAS DONE by Executive action alone ran simultaneously with the legislative proposals President Kennedy made to Congress. The first of these was drawn from a task-force report prepared under the supervision of Senator Paul H. Douglas and addressed to the problem of relieving distress in areas of chronic unemployment. It called for prompt legislative action to provide technical assistance, loans for private projects, loans and grants for public facilities, and training and retraining programs to provide new industry, new jobs and new growth. Mr. Kennedy threw his full weight behind these proposals, and in the end Congress approved of them in substantially the form desired by the President.

The calendar dates help to tell the story of many other things on the move:

February 6. President Kennedy sent to Congress a bill to authorize a temporary program of additional unemployment compensation to workers who had exhausted their state benefits. Another bill sent on the same day authorized Federal financial participation for a temporary period in state aid to needy children of unemployed parents.

February 7. President Kennedy sent to Congress a bill to extend the coverage of the Fair Labor Standards Act and to increase the minimum wage.

February 9. President Kennedy sent to Congress a special message on health and hospital care that dealt with all facets of the problem.

February 13. President Kennedy sent Congress a bill specifically designed to provide health insurance benefits for the aged, financed through the social-security system.

February 16. President Kennedy sent to Congress a bill to provide a special emergency program for feed grains.

February 20. President Kennedy sent to Congress a bill designed to improve the social-security program by broadening its coverage and liberalizing its benefits. He also sent to Congress a special message on education, outlining the terms of a comprehensive program of Federal assistance to public elementary and secondary schools; to college and university facilities; to college and university students; and to vocational education.

February 23. President Kennedy sent to Congress a special message on natural resources, detailing a co-ordinated Federal approach to the use of water resources; to "new starts" in power projects; to the control of water and air pollution; to the conversion of saline and brackish water; to the conservation of our forests; to the use of public lands; to the exploration of ocean resources; to the development of recreational areas.

February 24. President Kennedy sent to Congress two more bills which dealt in specific form with the expansion of medical resources and facilities.

February 28. President Kennedy sent to Congress a special message on highways, detailing the imminent collapse of the Federal "pay-as-you-go" Highway Program, and specifying the means for a timely completion of the full program authorized in 1956.

March 9. President Kennedy sent to Congress a special message on housing and community development, detailing new measures that would provide better housing for moderate-income families; for low-income families; for elderly people; for veterans; for the rehabilitation and conservation of residential areas; and for the development of community facilities and urban transportation.

TO BE SURE, there is a wide chasm to be bridged before such Presidential legislative recommendations are transformed into bills placed on the President's desk for his signature. Indeed, as is generally true of most Presidents, the fate of Mr. Kennedy's program will not be fully known until the last months of a legislative session or even of a Congress. Yet even if President Kennedy meets—as he has already met—a setback here and there, the paramount fact remains that he has placed his

Presidential banner at the head of the fight, using every legal and extra-legal resource at his command to win the maximum number of objects in the end.

Meanwhile, within the sphere of things where the Executive is free to act on its own, no corner of American life was left untouched by a new beginning of some sort. Even the Post Office Department, thanks to the new Postmaster General, J. Edward Day, is astir with a new spirit and a new sense of values. The policy of using experts from within the government—as for example, research specialists from the Bureau of Standards—was adopted in preference to the high costs of outside consultants in all phases of postal operations. Industry was invited to develop machines and methods for mail movement on its own, in preference to government investment in speculative research. The pornography museum of the Post Office Department was closed; the new emphasis, instead, was on enforcing pornography laws and regulations. So also the policy was established of cutting commemorative stamps from the forty-two issued in 1960 to a maximum of fifteen a year. And so on and on.

Yet all that was proposed or done on the domestic front, either by Executive Order or by legislation, was overshadowed by President Kennedy's conduct in the field of national security.

He inherited a government in which high-ranking military officers had grown used to issuing pronouncements on diplomatic and security policies, however embarrassing the consequences to their civilian superiors. President Kennedy lost no time in reasserting the Constitutional principle of civil supremacy. He made it plain that the voice of America, addressing the world, would be the voice of the duly elected President of the United States and not of a self-appointed President. He also made it plain that high-ranking military officers would be encouraged to state their professional views in the strongest possible terms within his personal hearing. They were also to be at liberty to answer the questions put to them at Congressional hearings. But once a Presidential decision was made, if they appealed to the public over the head of the President, their next act would be to comply with his request to turn in their uniforms.

President Kennedy also inherited a Pentagon whose internal wars were more ferocious than any war the United States is likely to wage against a foreign foe. Interservice rivalries, rivalries between Congressmen with Pentagon interests, rivalries between defense contractors with weapon systems to sell—all of which were further entangled with pet theories about how strong the Russians were—led to a grab-bag budget. Yet the budget is everything in defense matters. It is supposed to mirror our own estimate of the strength, capabilities and likely intentions of our prospective adversaries; it is also supposed to mirror our strategic military policy and the tactical means for executing it. As President Kennedy saw the matter, it mirrored organized confusion instead.

Thus, as a necessary first step to bring order out of chaos, President Kennedy directed Defense Secretary McNamara to make a thorough investigation of America's defense picture and to recommend what should be done to strengthen it.

When his report came by the end of February, it was examined in general terms at a White House meeting between President Kennedy, Special Counsel Sorensen, Budget Director Bell, Special Assistant for National Security Affairs Bundy, scientific advisor Wiesner, Secretary of Defense McNamara, Under Secretary of Defense Roswell L. Gilpatric, and Comptroller of the Defense Department Charles J. Hitch.

There was a more detailed examination at a subsequent White House meeting where the same men, except for President Kennedy, were present. Here, with Sorensen in the lead, the Defense Department representatives were asked to explain line by line what each of their budget requests actually represented. On this basis, Sorensen subsequently isolated the issues to be faced by President Kennedy, and private discussions between the pair led to still another meeting, presided over by Mr. Kennedy, where views were exchanged between White House staff members and the Defense Department representatives. Some decisions were tentatively made at this time; others were left in suspense for a thrashing-out between the President and Sorensen in a round of informal talks. In the end, however, President Kennedy alone made all the decisions that were crowded into the defense message he sent to the Congress on March 28.

The message had a strong affirmative tone. By its terms, the U.S. strategic nuclear force was to remain the cornerstone of national security. But it was the plain intention of President Kennedy to make that nuclear force less vulnerable, more reliable and—when coupled with an expanded and modernized conventional force—more versatile.

Among other things, for example, the message called for a step-up in the number and delivery dates of Polaris submarines; an increase in the production of solid-fuel Minute Men; an increase in SAC's capacity to maintain an around-the-clock airborne alert; a sharp boost in the number of long-range planes for airlift; an increase in sealift and technical aircraft; and the development of a safe warning system so that our retaliatory power would not rest on judgments made under ambiguous circumstances. Where the message called for cuts in the Eisenhower defense budget, the action was justified primarily on the ground that technological advances had rendered obsolete a number of existing programs the preceding Administration seemed prepared to continue.

WHILE THESE measures were being framed on the military front, onrushing events on the diplomatic front demanded the daily attention of the new President. He had long before concluded that the American people will stand behind their government in the face of any challenge as long as they feel confident that the President, and those he has named to positions of responsibility, know what they are getting into and how to get out of it. He had also concluded privately that his ceaseless task was to consolidate the public's trust in his capacity to manage the problems of war and peace in a calm but firm way. A single misstep in the beginning—amid the explosive situations he inherited from the Eisenhower Presidency—could lead to a loss of trust that would be fatal to his own Presidency and hence fatal to the nation.

Deliberately he had focused his Inaugural Address solely on the problems of world peace and the desire of the United States to do all that need be done to achieve a world-wide rule of law based on the consent of people everywhere. And again, just ten days later, in his State of the Union Message, he placed the search for peace at the center of the problems he had inherited. "I feel I must inform the Congress," he said, "that our analyses over the last ten days makes it clear that—in each of the principal areas of crisis—the tide of events has been running out and time has not been our friend." What could he do? In a race against time, he could try to establish positions from which he could hope first to dam the adverse tide and then turn it in the free world's favor.

The postscript to this line of reasoning took many forms. There was an emergency airlift of food to the Congo, an emergency relief program for Cuban refugees, and a new approach to the question of "colonialism" where our NATO allies were concerned. There was the outline of a new approach to a negotiated control of nuclear arms. There was the proposal for a new foreign-aid program that consolidated all existing programs and gave them the coherent meaning they lacked. There was a major Food for Peace program, the stirring new invention of the Peace Corps, and the outline of a new program for the development of Latin America.

Here, in this connection, President Kennedy brought to maturity the conviction that the provision of money, food, medicine and especially the provision of arms are not enough to rescue great masses of people from the corrosive bite of mass poverty. The nations receiving U. S. help must accept an obligation of their own to introduce a larger degree of social justice in their own affairs, to execute agrarian reforms, to increase the literacy of their people and to bring into being efficient and responsible instruments of public administration. Only by such means can the have-not nations escape the pattern of violent change by revolution and enter the safer path of progress by evolution.

The fund of public trust President Kennedy rapidly built up by all these new beginnings was put to a trial by fire in the Laotian crisis—and stood firm in his favor. The crisis was one he inherited from the Eisenhower Presidency. Yet he refused to take the easy political way out by saying that since he had not been a party to its start, he had no responsibility to deal with it as it grew more menacing.

In his first days in the White House he met seven times with his advisers for long reviews of measures

that could check a threatened explosion in all of southeast Asia. After that, he was the first to warn publicly that if the Communist expansionist thrust in Laos was not checked, the momentum of the thrust could shatter other nations in the area as well as elsewhere in the world. There was no bombast or bluster in this warning. Yet it was backed up by quiet moves that could give force, if necessary, to the words "Turn off the heat" imparted by Secretary of State Dean Rusk to Soviet Foreign Minister Andrei Gromyko at their State Department meeting.

The President had already given orders that would send a token Marine force to Thailand. Moves had been started that would bring Britain's Prime Minister Macmillan to a meeting with Mr. Kennedy in Key West. The French objections to the possible military involvement of SEATO forces had been anticipated and to some extent modified with a personal Presidential communication to Premier de Gaulle. The personal support of India's Prime Minister Nehru had been sought and granted. The free-world allied coalition had been alerted and solidly aligned behind President Kennedy's position. All that the President and his advisers could do had been done or was in the process of being done to improve the prospects of a peaceful solution. The nation knew that this was so and, as a result, was prepared to back him to the limit in the event that the promise of a peaceful solution proved in the end to be a false dawn.

So NOW the first hundred days are over; and in Mr. Kennedy's ceaseless new beginnings the time has come for yet another new beginning. No one can say for certain what the end will be. Yet with the recent past in mind, it seems fair to predict how Mr. Kennedy will conduct himself in the face of whatever the future proves to be. He will conduct himself like the President of the United States he called for in January 1960, when it seemed doubtful whether it would ever be his personal fortune to fill to the brim the dimensions of the role he described. He will conduct himself, that is, in ways that will continue to lend their own integrity to the integrity of the democratic political process.

Secretary of the Interior Udall, at the Sal River (Arizona) Reservation, talks with a squaw and the inspector from the local Indian Affairs Agency.

As President Kennedy has pointed out, there are 4,000 Navajo children like the 13-year-old girl above who have no school facilities. For the younger children (left) there are schools on the reservation.

OVERLEAF
Dawn at the site of the Glen Canyon Dam (Page, Arizona)

"The energy, the faith, the devotion which we bring to this endeavor will light our country and all who serve it—and the glow from that fire can truly light the world."

R. Sargent Shriver talks with interested students.

THE PEACE CORPS

"Our generation has been frustrated in wanting to participate in foreign affairs, but we have had no outlet. The Peace Corps gives us a chance to go out and solve the problems we hear so much about day by day."

"The Peace Corps will provide a chance for actual contact and involvement in national affairs in a personal and significant way."

"Students are frightened of a nuclear war, and now feel they can do something directly to prevent one through the Peace Corps."

"The Peace Corps can create good will for the United States by working mutually with peoples, rather than working at them. In the last few years students have become more interested in political activity. The Peace Corps is the only opportunity they have had to be actively involved up to now."

"Joining the Peace Corps is a much sounder proposal than joining the army and learning to use a rifle and dig trenches. In the Peace Corps you can use your knowledge of people and cultures, all the things you have learned in college, and put your education to work constructively."

"All of a sudden the youth of America has been awakened, an awakening which started with the sit-in movement. Students are finally realizing they have a place in society. Here is an opportunity not to change the world, necessarily, but to make it a better place."

On the next two pages, a portion of the Peace Corps Volunteer Application of William Cogswell, twenty years old, of Liberty, New York. A few years ago he made an 8,000-mile tour of the United States in a Model-A Ford. His enjoyment of traveling and pride in his knowledge of dairy farming give him a strong inclination to get out of Liberty and teach in India or Africa.

Indicate the degree of your skill with the following tools or equipment by placing a check in the appropriate box if you have the specified skill. Leave the box blank if you do not have the skill. If you check the first column for any item, do not check the second column for the same item.

15. Check as applicable to indicate your participation in the following activit for any one activity you check Column #2, please leave Column #1 bl that activity.

Sufficient to earn a living	Skilled amateur	
1 ☑	2 ☐	1. Tractor
1 ☑	2 ☐	2. Farm equipment
1 ☑	2 ☐	3. Bulldozer
1 ☐	2 ☐	4. Inboard power boat
1 ☐	2 ☐	5. Tools used by automobile mechanic
1 ☐	2 ☑	6. Tools used by carpenter
1 ☐	2 ☐	7. Tools used by surveyor
1 ☐	2 ☐	8. Tools used by plumber
1 ☐	2 ☐	9. Tools used by electrician
1 ☐	2 ☐	10. Tools used by mason
1 ☐	2 ☑	11. Tools used in metal working trades
1 ☐	2 ☐	12. Canning equipment
1 ☐	2 ☐	13. Handicrafters equipment
1 ☐	2 ☐	14. Chemical laboratory equipment
1 ☐	2 ☐	15. Biological laboratory equipment
1 ☐	2 ☐	16. Nursing equipment
1 ☐	2 ☐	17. Radio transmission and receiver equipment
1 ☑	2 ☐	18. Other. Specify Vet. work on cattle

List the specific tools or equipment in which you have the greatest skill.

farm equipment - Bulldozer - Vet. work
on cattle - Drugs, Syringes, udder infussion
needles
All small But important work on calf delivery

Indicate, for each of the following areas or countries, the extent of your knowledge of the area's or country's culture, history, and social or economic conditions. In indicating your knowledge, write the number of the appropriate code statement in the box preceding every cou

CODE

1. I know the area (or years.

2. I know the area (or years.

3. I know the area (or several months.

4. I know the area (or brief trips to it.

5. I have little or no kn

5	country or co
5	country or co
5	country or co
5	country or co
5	country or co
5	country or co
5	country or co
5	country or co
	country or co
5	country or co

Exu Facts

List the coun

or more mon

#1 I participate for an average of at least 2 hours per week | #2 I am recognized by others as highly skilled

#1	#2	
1 ☐	2 ☑	Track
1 ☐	2 ☑	Football
1 ☐	2 ☐	Swimming
1 ☐	2 ☑	Camping
1 ☐	2 ☐	Mountain Climbing
1 ☐	2 ☑	Hunting
1 ☐	2 ☐	Working with youth groups. Specify _____
1 ☐	2 ☐	Working as a volunteer in a hospital or clinic
1 ☐	2 ☐	Radio, electrical, automotive, carpentry, metal shop
1 ☐	2 ☐	Golf
1 ☐	2 ☑	Baseball
1 ☐	2 ☑	Bowling
1 ☑	2 ☐	Basketball
1 ☐	2 ☐	Skiing
1 ☐	2 ☐	Boxing
1 ☐	2 ☐	Wrestling
1 ☐	2 ☐	Boating
1 ☐	2 ☑	Hiking
1 ☐	2 ☑	Fishing
1 ☐	2 ☐	Leading group singing
1 ☐		Folk dancing
	2 ☐	Leading discussion groups
	2 ☐	Leading or participating in civic g
	2 ☐	Acting in or directing stage, radio
	2 ☐	Photography
	2 ☐	Playing a musical instrument
	2 ☐	Tennis
	2 ☐	Ice Hockey

ave you ever been discharged or resigned from any j sidered that your conduct or work was not satisfactor

1 ☐ Yes   2 ☑ No

answer is "Yes", give the details including the name proximate date of leaving and reasons in each case on estion 16.

you have any of the following physical or mental ail

☐ Yes. Specify which ailments_____

☑ No.

berculosis; Heart Disease; Diabetes; Cancer; Chror cluding polio); Stomach, liver or major intestinal tr lsions; Any other nervous or mental disorder; Drug o nt, or other deformity; Loss of a kidney; Asthma; L e trouble not correctable by glasses; Severe allergy.

you often need medical services, dental services, or a

☐ Yes. Specify _____

☑ No.

Code Number

4 -12

J. Binghampton
City

Write clearly

PEACE CORPS VOLUNTEER QUESTIONNAIRE

Name Cogswell   William   Charles
(Print)   (Last)   (First)   (Middle)   (Maiden)

sent address   91 Wawanda Avenue
Liberty   New York

(Month)   (Day)   (Year)   Remaining
until what date?

manent (home) address   91 Wawanda Ave.
Liberty   New York

941   Year of birth

n available for service in the Peace Corps.

☑ On and after this June 15.

	(Do not write in this space.)
1	Ref.
2	Med.
3	S.
4	MS.

11. If you do not know any foreign language, check here ☑ and go on to the next question. For th
following languages indicate your abilities by placing a check in each appropriate box. Check th
appropriate box only if you have the ability described at the head of the column for each of th
languages listed below. Mark your checks clearly.

	Give a short talk about the United	Read a news-	Understand a discussion between citizens of
Write a			

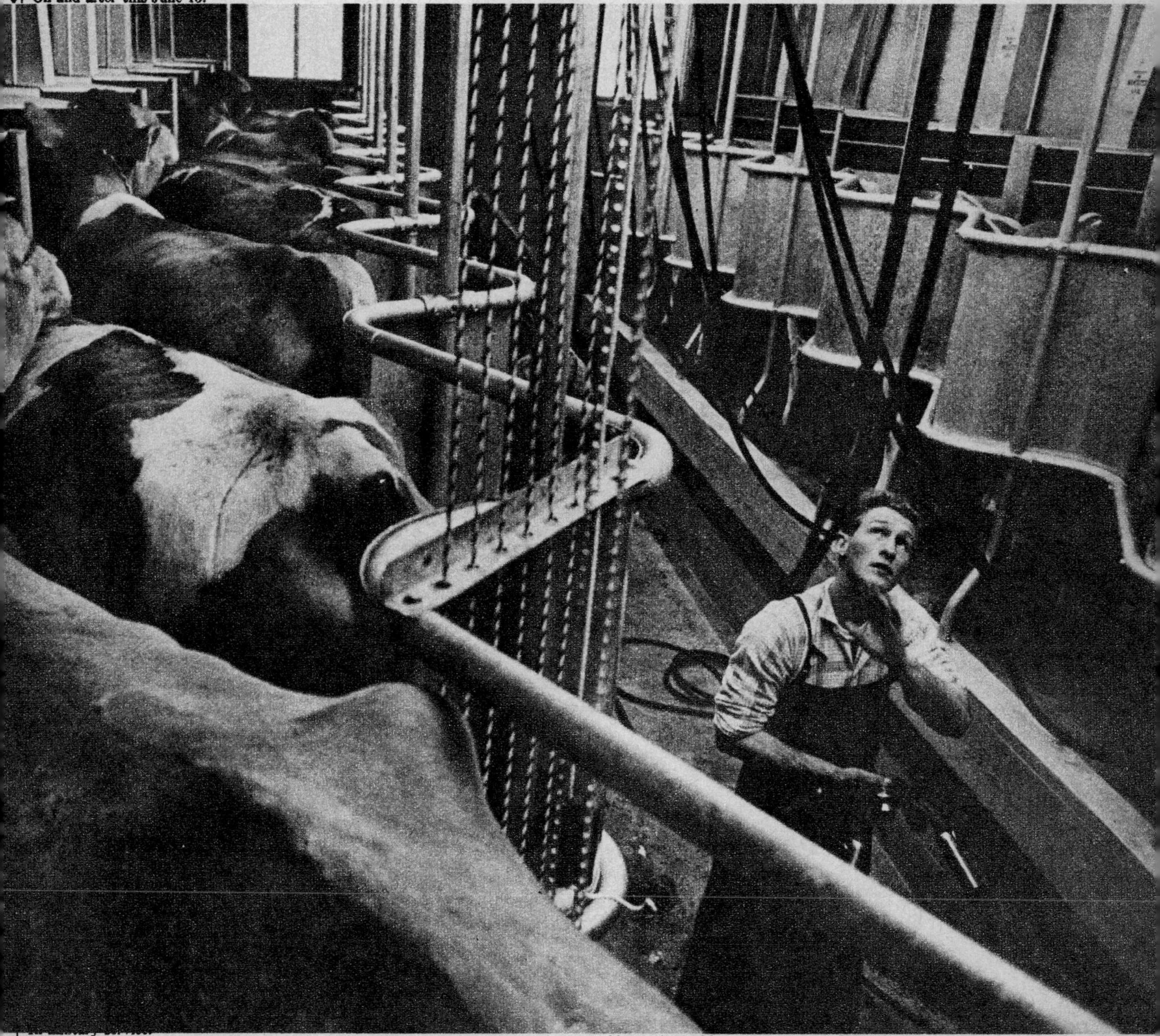

☐ Housewife.

☐ Other. Specify #2 Taking progams
At Cornell - Artificial
Breeding

If you checked box 2 for any area above give your reasons

137

"But let us begin."

Robert Weaver, Administrator of the Housing Home Finance Agency

Pierre Salinger, President Kennedy's Press Secretary

Edward R. Murrow, Director of the United States Information Agency

Abraham Ribicoff, Secretary of Health, Education and Welfare

Theodore Sorensen, Special Counsel to the President

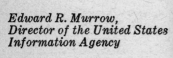

McGeorge Bundy, Special Assistant to the President

Jerome Wiesner,
Science Adviser
to President Kennedy

Roving Ambassador Averell Harriman
en route from Bonn to Paris

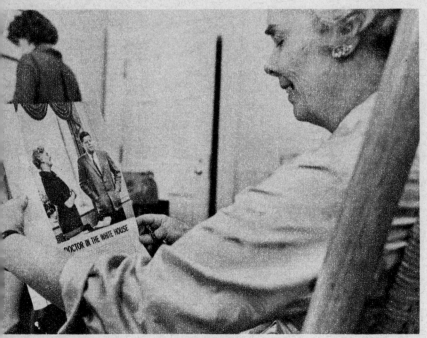

Dr. Janet Travell, Personal Physician to the President

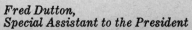

Arthur Schlesinger, Jr.,
Special Assistant to the President

Fred Dutton,
Special Assistant to the President

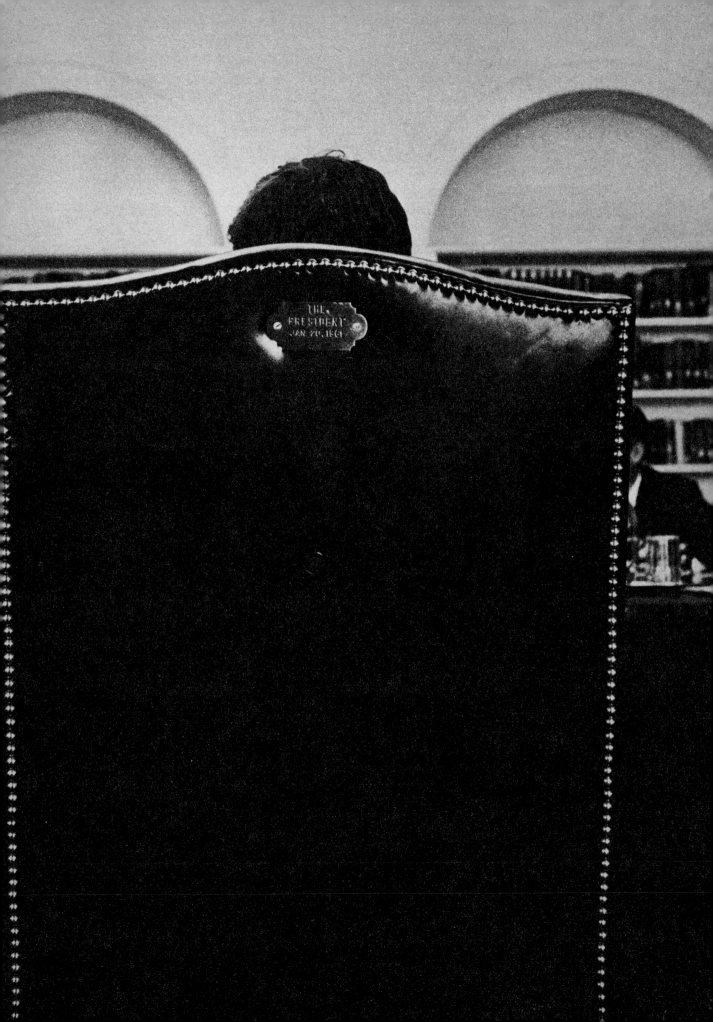

AND, AS THE FIRST HUNDRED DAYS WERE ENDING, the crisis, which had been a reasonable expectation from the beginning, given the world's universal turmoil of fear and hope, had become a fact. But the crisis that has come seems especially designed to test to the limit the confidence and coolness of the new Administration.

When, on April 17, Cuban rebels, with some backing from the United States, attempted to establish a beachhead in Cuba, in the name of freedom and of the revolution which Castro had perverted, they proved to have insufficient strength to accomplish the thrust. Local support was lacking. The whole operation was in any case on a very modest scale, resembling the effort made by Castro against Batista in 1956, which also ended in failure to hold a beachhead and sent the Castro men into hiding in the hills.

But the venture fell out of perspective. Castro denounced it as a full-scale American-backed invasion. American newspapers gave it front billing as the beginning of the end of Castro. The General Assembly of the United Nations was in session, acting as an inevitable sounding board for Cuba's frantic denunciations of the "American plot." In these conditions, the failure of a small group of freedom fighters in the face of overwhelming odds became the world's central preoccupation and has faced the President with his worst dilemma since he took office.

He seems to confront two almost opposite pressures. Inside America, the snubs and humiliations hurled at the "Yankees" by Castro, culminating in the failure of the invasion, have brought American public opinion some degrees closer to flash point. Voices are raised urging that Castro, as a small, squalid nuisance, be snuffed out. "Send the Marines in" expresses the anger and frustration of a nation already deeply perturbed by Communism's expanding power and inevitably conscious of its own vis-à-vis Castro.

But Communism has to be resisted not only in the small, vulnerable island in the Caribbean; it has to be contained throughout the emergent continents—in Asia, in Africa, above all in Latin America. In these lands, memories of colonialism, of economic dependence, of past examples of Western highhandedness, create a climate of opinion almost wholly opposed to violent, unilateral American intervention to end Castro's regime. An unimportant segment of American opinion thus presses for a solution which the areas most under Communist pressure reject. And the risk is that if the mood of hitting out and ending the local Communist nuisance in Cuba prevails, the President's power to combat Communism elsewhere will be dangerously weakened.

This is first of all a risk in the vital area of propaganda. In the world-wide battle for men's minds, Communism has the initial advantage of speaking the language of anti-imperialism—which is the language the emergent want to hear. During the Cuban crisis, the Communists pulled out all the organ stops of anti-colonialism. Every effort was made to revive memories of Western intervention, every opportunity seized to contrast "peace-loving Communists" with the "aggressive forces of Yankee imperialism." And the emergent lands responded with almost universal condemnation.

This extreme excitability of world opinion over the colonial issue cannot be shrugged off as sheer sentiment. It contains a down-to-earth military risk as well. Communism's technique in the uncommitted areas is centered on the small, nibbling guerrilla war. In this kind of struggle, local opinion and support are the key to victory. But if Communism can appropriate all the anticolonial slogans, local opinion may swing irretrievably away from the West. Then "sending the Marines into Cuba" would cut off one Communist Hydra head in the Caribbean only to create twenty more in Latin America or wherever else the struggle is joined.

Thus the hundred days end in a profound challenge to the levelheadedness and vision of the President and his Administration—and beyond them to the steadiness of free public opinion in the United States.

—BARBARA WARD

The Authors and

MARTIN AGRONSKY began his career as a writer on *The Palestine Post,* Israel's English-language daily, but has been a Washington correspondent since 1943. Prior to his radio and television assignment in the capital he reported for NBC from the Balkans, Africa, Singapore, Australia and Italy. In 1952 he was given the George Foster Peabody award for his "penetrating analyses of highly controversial matters."

CORNELL CAPA, photographic editor and moving force behind *Let Us Begin,* is a former *Life* staff photographer. In addition to a wide range of photographic essays, he has published several books, including *Retarded Children Can Be Helped* (with Maya Pines), *Through Gates of Splendor* and *Savage My Kinsman.* He was the winner of the Page One Award Citation and is a trustee of the American Society of Magazine Photographers.

BURT GLINN has covered a wide variety of news and feature stories throughout the Northwest and Alaska. He has been to Israel to cover the UN Truce Team Under Fire (1956), the Sinai campaign, the evacuation of refugees from Egypt (1957), and the filming of *Exodus.* In 1960 he was awarded the Mathew Brady Trophy and the title "Magazine Photographer of the Year."

HENRI CARTIER-BRESSON is one of the most renowned men in his field. He has been a photographer since 1931, and his work has been exhibited in the major museums of the world. His books, which have been published in a number of countries, include *The Decisive Moment, The People of Moscow, China* and *The Europeans.* With Robert Capa, David Seymour and George Rodger he founded the cooperative photographic agency Magnum, of which he is now chairman.

ERIC F. GOLDMAN is Professor of History at Princeton and the author of two major books in his field, *Rendezvous with Destiny* and *Crucial Decade,* as well as several textbooks in wide use, including *The World's History.* Professor Goldman is the moderator of the award-winning television show *The Open Mind* and also serves as a consultant to The Fund for the Republic.

ELLIOTT ERWITT joined Magnum in 1953 after service in France as U.S. Army Signal Corps photographer and free-lance work in Hollywood, New York and Pittsburgh. He has done extensive advertising campaigns for the Commonwealth of Puerto Rico, the French Tourist Office, the Chase Manhattan Bank, and IBM. Recent news assignments include coverage of the 1960 Democratic Convention, the Kennedy Inauguration and the seizure of the *Santa Maria.*

SIDNEY HYMAN, whose forthcoming book *Eisenhower: Promise and Performance* will be published in the fall, is also the author of *The American Presidency.* With Marriner Eccles he also wrote *Beckoning Frontiers.* Mr. Hyman is a regular contributor to *The New York Times Magazine, The Reporter, The Saturday Review* and *Harper's* and is a consultant to Encyclopaedia Britannica.

Editorial assistants: DORIS ANTHONY, EDITH CAPA

Photographers

DENNIS STOCK joined Magnum in 1951, after winning first prize in *Life*'s Young Photographers Contest. Most of his assignments have related to the performing arts (Audrey Hepburn, Igor Stravinsky, Marlon Brando and James Dean). He has also worked as film-dialogue coach, second unit director, and television producer. His book *Jazz Street*, published in 1960, was termed by the New York *Times* one of the hundred best books of the year.

CONSTANTINE MANOS was hired at nineteen as the official photographer of the Boston Symphony Orchestra. He served two years in the Army as staff photographer for *Stars and Stripes* in Europe, and returned to free-lance magazine photography in New York, where he published his work in *Life, Coronet, Esquire* and *Pageant*. His photographic book, *Portrait of a Symphony*, was published in the fall of 1960.

NICOLAS TIKHOMIROFF, following a brief training as a journalist, worked as a photographic apprentice, then did fashion assignments for Marie-France in Paris. Since 1955 he has worked for Telephoto news agency, free-lanced on projects from Russia to Hawaii, worked for Rapho-Guillemette and then *Jours de France*, principally on news coverage. He is a recent member of Magnum and has covered Algeria and Laos.

INGE MORATH has done photojournalism in the Middle East, South Africa, Europe and Mexico, publishing her photographs in several books, among them *From Persia to Iran, Venice Observed* and *Fiesta in Pamplona*. She is known for her photographs of personalities like Henry Moore and Picasso. Her most recent book is *Bring Forth the Children*, done in conjunction with Yul Brynner.

BARBARA WARD is the foreign-affairs editor of *The Economist* of London and the author of six books: *The West at Bay, Policy for the West, Faith and Freedom, Interplay of East and West, Five Ideas That Change the World* and the current *India and the West*. Miss Ward, who holds honorary doctorates from Fordham, Smith, Columbia and Harvard, is currently lecturing at the Radcliffe Graduate School.

MARC RIBOUD, who was formerly an industrial engineer in Lyons, joined Magnum in 1953. Since that time he has covered stories ranging from the Conservative Party Conference in London to an overland trip from Paris to Calcutta and going on to China, Alaska, Russia, Algiers and the whole continent of Africa. His book *Femmes du Japon* was published in Paris in 1958.

IRA WOLFERT served as a combat correspondent in both the Pacific and European theaters during World War II and won the Pulitzer Prize for his dispatches from Guadalcanal. His books include three novels, *Tucker's People, Married Men* and *An Act of Love*, and three works of non-fiction, *Battle of the Solomons, American Guerrilla in the Philippines* and *An Epidemic of Genius*.

Design and production: HELEN BARROW

THE
INAUGURAL ADDRESS

January 20, 1961

WE OBSERVE today not a victory of party but a celebration of freedom—symbolizing an end as well as a beginning — signifying renewal as well as change. For I have sworn before you and Almighty God the same solemn oath our forebears prescribed nearly a century and three-quarters ago.

The world is very different now. For man holds in his mortal hands the power to abolish all forms of human poverty and all forms of human life. And yet the same revolutionary beliefs for which our forebears fought are still at issue around the globe—the belief that the rights of man come not from the generosity of the state but from the hand of God.

We dare not forget today that we are the heirs of that first revolution. Let the word go forth from this time and place, to friend and foe alike, that the torch has been passed to a new generation of Americans—born in this century, tempered by war, disciplined by a hard and bitter peace, proud of our ancient heritage—and unwilling to witness or permit the slow undoing of those human rights to which this nation has always been committed, and to which we are committed today at home and around the world.

Let every nation know, whether it wishes us well or ill, that we shall pay any price, bear any burden, meet any hardship, support any friend, oppose any foe to assure the survival and the success of liberty.

This much we pledge—and more.

To those old allies whose cultural and spiritual origins we share, we pledge the loyalty of faithful friends. United, there is little we cannot do in a host of new co-operative ventures. Divided, there is little we can do—for we dare not meet a powerful challenge at odds and split asunder.

To those new states whom we welcome to the ranks of the free, we pledge our word that one form of colonial control shall not have passed away merely to be replaced by a far more iron tyranny. We shall not always expect to find them supporting our view. But we shall always hope to find them strongly supporting their own freedom—and to remember that, in the past, those who foolishly sought power by riding the back of the tiger ended up inside.

To those peoples in the huts and villages of half the globe struggling to break the bonds of mass misery, we pledge our best efforts to help them help themselves, for whatever period is required—not because the Communists may be doing it, not because we seek their votes, but because it is right. If a free society cannot help the many who are poor, it cannot save the few who are rich.

TO OUR SISTER REPUBLICS south of our border, we offer a special pledge—to convert our good words into good deeds—in a new alliance for progress—to assist free men and free governments in casting off the chains of poverty. But this peaceful revolution of hope cannot become the prey of hostile powers. Let all our neighbors know that we shall join with them to oppose aggression or subversion anywhere in the Americas. And let every other power know that this hemisphere intends to remain the master of its own house.

To that world assembly of sovereign states, the United Nations, our last best hope in an age where the instruments of war have far outpaced the instruments of peace, we renew our pledge of support—to prevent it from becoming merely a forum for invective — to strengthen its shield of the new and the weak—and to enlarge the area in which its writ may run.

Finally, to those nations who would make themselves our adversary, we offer not a pledge but a request: that both sides begin anew the quest for peace, before the dark powers of destruction unleashed by science engulf all humanity in planned or accidental self-destruction.

We dare not tempt them with weakness. For only when our arms are sufficient beyond doubt can we be certain beyond doubt that they will never be employed. *12*

But neither can two great and powerful groups of nations take comfort from our present course—both sides overburdened by the cost of modern weapons, both rightly alarmed by the steady spread of the deadly atom, yet both racing to alter that uncertain balance of terror that stays the hand of mankind's final war. *13*

So let us begin anew—remembering on both sides that civility is not a sign of weakness, and sincerity is always subject to proof. Let us never negotiate out of fear. But let us never fear to negotiate. *14*

Let both sides explore what problems unite us instead of belaboring those problems which divide us. *15*

Let both sides, for the first time, formulate serious and precise proposals for the inspection and control of arms—and bring the absolute power to destroy other nations under the absolute control of all nations. *16*

Let both sides seek to invoke the wonders of science instead of its terrors. Together let us explore the stars, conquer the deserts, eradicate disease, tap the ocean depths and encourage the arts and commerce. *17*

Let both sides unite to heed in all corners of the earth the command of Isaiah—to "undo the heavy burdens... [and] let the oppressed go free." *18*

And if a beachhead of cooperation may push back the jungles of suspicion, let both sides join in creating a new endeavor—not a new balance of power, but a new world of law, where the strong are just and the weak secure and the peace preserved. *19*

A<small>LL THIS</small> will not be finished in the first 100 days. Nor will it be finished in the first 1,000 days, nor in the life of this Administration, nor even perhaps in our lifetime on this planet. But let us begin. *20*

In your hands, my fellow citizens, more than mine, will rest the final success or failure of our course. Since this country was founded, each generation of Americans has been summoned to give testimony to its national loyalty. The graves of young Americans who answered the call to service surround the globe. *21*

Now the trumpet summons us again—not as a call to bear arms, though arms we need—not as a call to battle, though embattled we are—but a call to bear the burden of a long twilight struggle year in and year out, "rejoicing in hope, patient in tribulation"—a struggle against the common enemies of man: tyranny, poverty, disease and war itself. *22*

Can we forge against these enemies a grand and global alliance, north and south, east and west, that can assure a more fruitful life for all mankind? Will you join in that historic effort? *23*

In the long history of the world, only a few generations have been granted the role of defending freedom in its hour of maximum danger. I do not shrink from this responsibility—I welcome it. I do not believe that any of us would exchange places with any other people or any other generation. The energy, the faith, the devotion which we bring to this endeavor will light our country and all who serve it—and the glow from that fire can truly light the world. *24*

A<small>ND SO</small>, my fellow Americans: ask not what your country can do for you—ask what you can do for your country. *25*

My fellow citizens of the world: ask not what America will do for you, but what together we can do for the freedom of man. *26*

Finally, whether you are citizens of America or citizens of the world, ask of us here the same high standards of strength and sacrifice which we ask of you. With a good conscience our only sure reward, with history the final judge of our deeds, let us go forth to lead the land we love, asking His blessing and His help, but knowing that here on earth God's work must truly be our own. *27*